Christian Menz

Explaining Croatia's (non)compliance with EU conditionality on ICTY cooperation

Do external incentives make the difference?

Anchor Academic Publishing

Menz, Christian: Explaining Croatia's (non)compliance with EU conditionality on ICTY cooperation: Do external incentives make the difference? Hamburg, Anchor Academic Publishing 2013

Buch-ISBN: 978-3-95489-183-2
PDF-eBook-ISBN: 978-3-95489-683-7
Druck/Herstellung: Anchor Academic Publishing, Hamburg, 2013

Bibliografische Information der Deutschen Nationalbibliothek:
Die Deutsche Nationalbibliothek verzeichnet diese Publikation in der Deutschen Nationalbibliografie; detaillierte bibliografische Daten sind im Internet über http://dnb.d-nb.de abrufbar.

Bibliographical Information of the German National Library:
The German National Library lists this publication in the German National Bibliography. Detailed bibliographic data can be found at: http://dnb.d-nb.de

Table of Contents

List of Acronyms

AFP	Agence France-Presse
BBC	British Broadcasting Corporation
BCHR	Belgrade Centre for Human Rights
BTI	Bertelsmann Transformation Index
CARDS	Community Assistance for Reconstruction, Development and Stabilization
CEE	Central and Eastern Europe
CFSP	Common Foreign and Security Policy
CNN	Cable News Network
DC	Democratic Center
DS	Democratic Party (*Demokratska Stranka*)
EBRD	European Bank for Reconstruction and Development
EIM	External Incentives Model
ENP	European Neighborhood Policy
EU	European Union
FRY	Federal Republic of Yugoslavia
FYROM	The Former Yugoslav Republic of Macedonia
GAERC	General Affairs and External Relations Council
HDSSB	Croatian Democratic Council of Slavonia and Baranya (*Hrvatski Demokratski Sabor Slavonije i Baranje)*
HDZ	Croatian Democratic Union (*Hratske Demokratska Zajednica*)
HND	Independent Croatian Democrats (*Hrvatski Nezavisni Demokrati*)
HNS	Croatian People's Party (*Hrvatska narodna stranka*)
HSLS	Croatian Social Liberal Party (*Hrvatska Socijalno-Liberalna Stranka*)
HSP	Croatian Party of Rights (*Hrvatska Stranka Prava)*
HSS	Croatian Peasant Party (*Hrvatska* Seljačka Stranka)
HSU	Croatian Party of Pensioners (*Hrvatska Stranka Umirovljenika*)
ICC	International Criminal Court
ICG	International Crisis Group
IDS	Istrian Democratic Assembly (*Istarski Demokratski Sabor*)
ICTY	International Criminal Tribunal for the former Yugoslavia
IMF	International Monetary Fund
IPA	Instrument for Pre-Accession
IR	International Relations
ISPA	Instrument for Structural Policies for Pre-Accession
KNS	Coalition of People's Agreement
LDP	Liberal Democratic Party (*Liberalno Demokratska Partija*)
LS	Liberal Party (*Liberalna Stranka*)
NATO	North Atlantic Treaty Organization
NYT	The New York Times
OSCE	Organization for Security and Co-operation in Europe
PfP	Partnership for Peace
PHARE	Poland and Hungary: Aid for Restructuring of the Economies
RA	Regional Approach
RFE/RL	Radio Free Europe / Radio Liberty
SAA	Stabilization and Association Agreement
SAP	Stabilization and Association Process
SAPARD	Special Accession Programme for Agriculture and Rural Development
SDP	Social Democratic Party of Croatia (*Socijaldemokratska Partija Hrvatske*)
UK	United Kingdom
UN	United Nations
UNDP	United Nations Development Program
UNSC	United Nations Security Council
US	United States
USA	United States of America
WB	Western Balkans

1. Introduction

For the positive experience with tying progress in negotiations with progress in reform in Central and Eastern Europe (CEE) the European Union (EU) made its membership offer to the Western Balkans (WB) countries conditional on specific democratic principles, most notably (full) cooperation with the International Criminal Tribunal for the former Yugoslavia (ICTY) and respect for the Dayton Peace Accord.[1] Yet, although EU membership is regarded as highly attractive both for political elites and the general public in the region, the erratic record of compliance with ICTY-related EU conditionality raises questions about the EU's ability to provide for 'rule transfer' and 'norm diffusion' in the current enlargement round and poses a puzzle to scholars of international relations and EU enlargement alike.

As I will demonstrate for the case of Croatia, both the Račan (2000-2003) and Sanader governments (since 2003) have seen many ups and downs of ICTY cooperation. The core question this study addresses is: What factors explain variation in Croatia's compliance with ICTY-related EU conditionality? The investigation period sets in with the democratic turn in 2000 and ends in December 2005, when the last remaining indictee left for The Hague. To provide for a systematic and theoretically informed analysis, the study will be oriented by the hypotheses and variables of the rationalist 'external incentives model' (EIM) (Schimmelfennig/Sedelmeier 2004; 2005a). The EIM has been labeled the "most refined theoretical approach" with the "strongest explanatory power" regarding EU 'rule transfer' to third countries (Trauner 2009: 776-777).[2] Schimmelfennig has already applied the EIM to the enlargement round in the WB, stating the model's "continuing relevance" based on hi findings that high and credible EU incentives as well as domestic adoption costs would still b the most important factors concerning compliance with EU conditionality (Schimmelfennig 2008: 918, 932-933). However, in his inquiries compliance with ICTY-related conditionality has been given limited attention only on a few pages as a (small) part of broader analyses (Schimmelfennig et al. 2006: 78-96; Schimmelfennig 2008). Moreover, in recent examinations it has been doubted whether the EIM as a rationalist model would be an adequate framework for the explanation of (non)compliance with ICTY conditionality (Freyburg/Richter 2010; Rajkovic 2007). Nonetheless, these studies – even though they refer to the EIM – build on research designs different from that of the EIM. Apart from that, there have been numerous examinations of ICTY cooperation of the concerned WB target states,

[1] Western Balkans is the official EU term for the countries of former Yugoslavia minus Slovenia, yet including Albania.

[2] Third country means any country that is not a member state of the European Union.

but for the most part they have not been theoretically informed and thus remained descriptive. For these reasons, the EIM will be taken as the overall framework for analysis.[3]

The theoretical part of this paper starts with a short general overview of the literature on external factors of democratization and their impact on the domestic level. Subsequently, the external governance approach will be outlined as an adequate concept to detect the mechanisms underlying EU policy transfer and norm diffusion to third countries. Moreover, the logics of rationalist and constructivist theoretical reasoning will be pointed out in order to illustrate the underlying assumptions of the EIM. Thereafter, the current state of empirical knowledge on (non)compliance with EU conditionality will be discussed and existing research gaps identified. The empirical section is guided by the assumptions of the EIM and uses process-tracing to identify crucial factors that could explain Croatia's inconsistent pattern of compliance with ICTY conditionality. In the conclusion, the main findings will be examined against the background of recent research on compliance with ICTY conditionality that at least partly rejects rationalist assumptions preferring constructivist reasoning instead.

2. Theoretical foundations and current state of research

2.1 Theory and development of hypotheses

2.1.1 The role of external factors in democratization research

Having turned more or less a blind eye to it before, in the beginning of the 1990s scholars in the field of democratization research started to take into account external factors (cf. Grugel 2005). However, "the international dimension of democracy promotion nonetheless remains at best understudied and poorly understood" (Schraeder 2003: 22). There is a lack of systematic, theory-driven research about the interaction and interdependence of internal and external factors as well as about under which conditions external actors are able to influence domestic reforms and 'transfer' their rules (cf. Magen/Morlino 2009: 11-12). The limited number of thorough empirical and theoretical studies on internal-external linkages of democracy promotion can partly be ascribed to the rather isolated disciplines of international relations (IR), comparative politics, institutionalism and international law which resulted in "largely separate, independent and self-contained spheres of inquiry" (Magen/Morlino 2009: 11). While IR scholars have often neglected the domestic scene, political comparativists have tended to fade out the role of external actors and ideas (cf. Flockhart 2005b: 2-10; Moravcsik

[3] Nonetheless, my goal is not to falsify the empirical validity of the EIM, since "contrary to naïve Falsificationism, no experiment, experimental report, observation statement or well-corroborated low-level falsifying hypothesis alone can lead to falsification" (Lakatos 1978: 35).

1993: 5-17; Whitehead 2004: 139-141; Yilmaz 2002; however see Cooley 2003; Levitsky/Lucan 2006). Concerning the latter, as a sub-discipline of comparative politics, the transition literature provided valuable input to the understanding of domestic democratization processes. It elaborated on crucial systemic factors for processes of liberalization, institutionalization and consolidation, such as the party system or the constitution (e.g. Birch 2003; von Beyme 2001; Bunce 2003; Elgie/Zielonka 2001). Moreover, important insights were provided on the political economy of negotiation processes between incumbent elites and reformers during regime change (e.g. Haggard/Kaufmann 1997; Przeworski 1991) and the significance of 'state-building' and 'nation-building' as a precondition for democratic consolidation (e.g. Linz/Stepan 1996). Regarding the links between the domestic and the international scene important contributions have been made within the IR discipline. The 'second-image reversed' theory[4] (Gourevitch 1978) from IR research has provided a highly valuable framework to study how systemic factors of the international system influence political outcomes at the level of nation states (cf. Pevehouse 2005: 4). Putnam (1988) finally combined the international and domestic scene in his 'two-level approach' which assumes that domestic actors have to calculate costs and benefits at different "playing fields" with different "win sets" both in international negotiations and in domestic politics. Nonetheless, the literature on external democracy promotion predominantly takes the point of view of those countries actively engaged in anchoring democracy abroad – their motives, instruments and strategies – rather than looking at the experiences and effects in the target states or the internal-external linkages of democracy promotion (cf. Magen/Morlino 2009: 12).

The recent eastern enlargement of the EU as a natural experiment enabled researchers to investigate the links between the domestic and international sphere in more detail. Yet although eastern enlargement has been subject to countless analyses, for to the most part they remained descriptive or methodologically weak (cf. Schimmelfennig/Sedelmeier 2005d: 4). Nonetheless, increasingly sophisticated book-length research projects helped to identify crucial variables which influence processes of EU 'rule transfer' to third states, be it via enlargement (Grabbe 2006; Kelley 2004a; Linden 2002; Schimmelfennig 2003; Schimmelfennig/Sedelmeier 2005a; Schimmelfennig et al. 2006; Vachudova 2005), in the context of pre-accession negotiations (Blockmans 2007; Richter 2009b) or via the European

[4] The abstract concept of the 'second-image-reversed' theory goes back to the 'three images' theory by Waltz (1959) who elaborated on the determinants of war. He distinguished between a first level of individual statesmen ("first image"), a second level of individual nation states ("second image") and a third international or "systemic" level (systemic causal factors, that is the "third image"). While Waltz elaborated on each of the three different causal mechanisms, the third image built the backbone of his argumentation. Gourevitch (1978), on the other hand, did not focus on domestic causes and international effects ("second image"), but instead on international causes and domestic effects ("second image reversed").

Neighbourhood Policy (ENP) (Emerson/Youngs 2009; Weber et al. 2007; Youngs 2008). However, it remains unclear to what extent the inferences drawn from these studies can be applied to other related subfields as they mostly focused on single enlargement rounds, policy areas, or single countries whereas "rigorous comparative analysis of the EU expansion-democratization nexus has remained sparse and fragmented" (Magen/Morlino 2009: 15).

2.1.2 The external governance approach

Most prominently the EU engages in non-member countries via enlargement, the Union' most successful foreign policy tool according to the Commission (2003: 5). However, enlargement policy as the main foreign policy instrument might recede into the background in light of the EU's limited 'integration capacity' and the small number of remaining European states eligible for membership. Furthermore, with the establishment of the EU's Common Foreign and Security Policy (CFSP) in the 1990s and the launch of the ENP at the Copenhagen European Council in 2002, the Union institutionalized its external relations with non-candidate countries that are perceived to affect the EU's stability, security and economic well-being. Therefore, in parallel, the 'external governance approach' has been developed which serves as an overall theoretical concept for the analysis of the EU's external action both toward countries with and without a membership perspective.[5] According to this concept, the EU tries to gradually 'externalize' its governance to non-member states in order to meet its functional needs and to achieve both internal and foreign policy goals (cf. Lavenex 2004: 681, 694). In the words of Sandra Lavenex "external governance takes place when parts of the *acquis communautaire* are extended to non-member states" (2004: 683). Renner, on the other hand, defined external governance as "the ability of an actor to influence the rules that govern social entities beyond its borders" (2009: 4). The concept of external governance focuses on characteristics of specific systems of rules and the function of these rules in the EU's external relations. It derives from the respective governance approaches in IR and comparative politics while, in contrast to traditional foreign policy analysis, it rejects the unified state actor model. Moreover, it neither focuses on countries nor regions as units of observation, but rather on multi-dimensional institutional processes of policy transfer and norm diffusion (cf. Lavenex/Schimmelfennig 2009: 794-795).

---

[5] Since the external governance approach tries to capture the whole compendium of EU external action across countries, regions or policy areas it also includes formal relations with third states beyond enlargement, e.g. in the context of the European Economic Area (cf. Lavenex 2004: 682-684). Moreover, not necessarily contractual relations are needed for the 'diffusion' or 'transfer' of rules, as it may happen either spontaneously in cases of high interdependence (cf. Lavenex/Schimmelfennig 2009: 79) or if third states regard certain EU rules as adequate for problem-solving and consequently adopt them by themselves.

Analytically, one can distinguish between two ideal types of external modes of governance: hierarchy and networks.[6] Hierarchical or "old" (Schimmelfennig/Sedelmeier 2004: 674) modes of external governance are characterized by top-down communication as well as fixed, legally constraining institutional templates, which third countries adopt within vertical processes of command and control, often by the use of conditionality (cf. Lavenex/Schimmelfennig 2009: 796-797).[7] "New" modes of governance via non-hierarchical networks, on the other hand, often include private actors and aim at the exchange of resources and/or trust (cf. Börzel 2009b; Héritier 2002; Scharpf 1997: 116-150). Therefore, the network mode of external governance is based on 'rule transfer' via learning and persuasion which makes it conducive to socialization processes (cf. Börzel 2006: 78-80; Börzel/Risse 2009; Checkel 1999, 2001; Schimmelfennig/Sedelmeier 2004: 673-675).[8] These networks favor horizontal, flexible, non-coercive institutions for coordination and often involve instruments such as financial assistance, benchmarking, naming and shaming or voluntary agreements.

However, the Commission as the main actor in enlargement policy predominantly only addressed governing elites whereas civil society or political (opposition) parties have not been subject of conditionality which suggests a predominance of 'old governance' modes (cf. Börzel 2009a; Grabbe 2006: 207-208; Pridham 2007: 449-450; Schimmelfennig/Sedelmeier 2004: 675; Wichmann 2007: 43-44).[9] On the other hand, since 2004, the Commission has repeatedly stressed the importance of an enhanced "civil society dialogue" to strengthen cooperation with non-state actors during the accession process (e.g. Commission 2005a: 4). Moreover, the European Parliament, the Council or even individual member states have increasingly gained influence on enlargement issues which placed political constraints on the Commission and politicized the enlargement negotiations (cf. Pridham 2007: 455; Sebastian 2008: 10; Youngs 2009: 896). This might suggest that, first, instruments of network governance might be more widely used, e.g. through inter-parliamentary commissions and, second, that politics of enlargement will become more similar to the EU's internal system of governance. Yet little knowledge exists on the impact of such changes on the EU's ability to

---

6 Schimmelfennig and Lavenex (2009: 796, 799) add a "market" mode of external governance, but since markets by definition act unintentionally, they qualify as nothing but a steering instrument (cf. Börzel 2006: 80).

7 In contrast to the EU's supranational 'community method' vis-à-vis its member states, non-member states are formally free to choose whether or not they want to subordinate to EU law. Practically, however, the power asymmetry between the EU and potential candidates often leads to "quasi-hierarchical" relationships which also are a necessary (but insufficient) condition for EU conditionality to be effective (cf. Börzel 2006: 86; Lavenex/Schimmelfennig 2009: 796; Moravcsik/Vachudova 2003).

8 In general, networks can be either (1) intergovernmental (involving public actors only), (2) social (only private actors), or (3) public-private (public and private actors cooperate on equal footing) (cf. Börzel 2006: 79).

9 Schimmelfennig et al. distinguished between an "intergovernmental channel" and a "transnational channel" (2003: 498): in the first case the EU addresses governments directly while in the latter it exerts influence via societal actors in non-member countries.

'externalize' its rules. To provide a better understanding scholars draw from 'compliance' or 'socialization' research which aim at demonstrating why actors do (not) comply with specific (international) rules (e.g. Checkel 2001; Börzel/Risse 2002; Flockhart 2005a; Kelley 2004a; Schimmelfennig 2003; Zürn/Checkel 2005). Socialization research is concerned with processes of adoption, application and internalization of international rules and norms. In compliance research the focus is laid on conditions and instruments which enable international actors to initiate sub-systemic and domestic reforms. Since this branch of research is based on rationalist and constructivist institutionalism, let us subsequently first single out the basic assumptions of the social meta-theories of rationalism and constructivism.

2.1.3 Basic concepts of rationalism and constructivism

In institutionalism, there is a paradigmatic conflict between rationalist and constructivist authors due to different assumptions derived from two basic logics of social action: while rationalists assume a 'logic of consequences', constructivists assume a 'logic of appropriateness' (cf. March/Olsen 1998: 949).[10] These ideal types translate into specific ontological premises such as that of an individualistic, materialist actor in rationalism who is calculating costs and benefits given his preferences and interests and his will to maximize his utility. To the contrary, in constructivism, actors rather follow a "social and ideational ontology" (Schimmelfennig/Sedelmeier 2005d: 11), i.e. actors are assumed to behave according to social and cultural norms, values and (socially constructed) identities (cf. Risse 2003: 107-110).[11] Furthermore, these premises very often determine the concrete research design as well as the use of specific theoretical models. Rationalists presuppose a logic of consequences investigating the 'externalization' of domestic rules and consequently favor policies that strive for changing cost-benefit-calculations through social (e.g. status, international recognition) or material (trade opportunities, financial assistance) incentives (e.g. Vachudova 2005: 63-79, 108-110). Usually, institutions are considered as intervening variables, which may alter individual cost-benefit calculations by offering additional incentives or constraints, but they do not generate changes of identity or interests (cf. Schimmelfennig/Sedelmeier 2005b: 10). By contrast, authors of constructivist institutionalism explain socialization through processes of institutionalization and habituation as well as through deliberative, communicative processes of argumentation and persuasion (e.g. Checkel

[10] This dispute marks the debate between rationalist institutionalism and sociological (constructivist) institutionalism in comparative politics as well as between rationalism and constructivism in IR theory.

[11] In the words of March and Olsen, "[h]uman actors are imagined to follow rules that associate particular identities to particular situations, approaching individual opportunities for action by assessing similarities between current identities and choice dilemmas and more general concepts of self and situations" (1998: 951).

1999, 2005a; Goodman/Jinks 2003; Risse 1999: 3).[12] Finally, rationalists usually regard rule adoption as sufficient for a successful socialization process as it implies a change of behavior (e.g. Schimmelfennig et al. 2006: 3-4). On the other hand, out of a constructivist perspective only a reflexive change of attitude provides for internalization of norms as the final stage of successful socialization process (cf. Checkel 2005a: 808-813; Flockhart 2005c: 52-59; Wendt 1999: 262-278, 285-290, 302-311; Zürn/Checkel 2005: 1053-1054).[13]

2.1.4 The external incentives model (EIM)

Schimmelfennig and Sedelmeier (2004, 2005a) developed the rationalist EIM which is based on material bargaining mechanisms and centered on actors who are "strategic utility-maximizers interested in the maximization of their own power and welfare" (2004: 663; also see 2005b: 10). The EIM assumes that EU conditionality follows the strategy of "reinforcement by reward": whether incentives will be rewarded or withheld is dependent on compliance, but neither extra costs will be inflicted ("reinforcement by punishment") nor unconditional assistance provided ("reinforcement by support") (ibid. 2004: 663-664, 2005b: 11). The core hypothesis of the EIM is that a target state adopts EU rules if the benefits of incentives surpass the 'domestic adoption costs'. The cost-benefit calculations are based on: "(i) the determinacy of conditions, (ii) the size and speed of rewards, (iii) the credibility of threats and promises, and (iv) the size of adoption costs" (ibid. 2004: 664, 2005b: 16). The size of adoption costs of a government is considered as crucial for the effectiveness of conditionality which depend on the preferences of both the government and of 'veto-players' (ibid. 2004: 666-667, 2005b: 16-17), that is "individual or collective actors whose agreement is necessary for a change of the status quo" (Tsebelis 2002: 19).[14] In addition to the EIM, Schimmelfennig and Sedelmeier (2005a) add two alternative models of external governance which are informed by constructivist theorizing and assume a logic of appropriateness: (1) the 'social learning model', which hypothesizes that "*a state adopts EU rules if it is persuaded of*

---

[12] According to the constructivist IR theory of 'deliberative/argumentative behavior' (which draws from Habermasian social theory) competing actors in discursive processes put aside their individual interest or preferences to agree on the "better argument" which shall then become the basis for subsequent action (cf. Risse 1999, 2003: 111-115).

[13] In the words of Finnemore and Sikkink, "rule internalization" has occurred once "norms acquire a taken- for granted quality and are no longer a matter of broad public debate" (1998: 895). Methodologically, however it is very difficult to detect that rule implementation and/or internalization have actually taken place (cf. Morlino/Magen 2009b: 242).

[14] The EIM's hypothesis on adoption costs reads: "[t]he likelihood of rule adoption decreases with the number of veto players incurring net adoption costs (opportunity costs, welfare, and power losses) from compliance" (Schimmelfennig/Sedelmeier 2005b: 17). Also see Engert (2003: 54) and Morlino/Magen (2009a: 44-45) who use very similar hypotheses in their analytical frameworks.

the appropriateness of EU rules" (ibid. 2004: 667-668, 2005b: 18-20); (2) the 'lesson-drawing model' assumes the actors' instrumental rationality while it holds that "a *state adopts EU rules, if it expects these rules to solve domestic policy problems effectively*" (ibid. 2004: 668, 2005b: 22-25).[15] According to the 'social learning model', (1) the greater the legitimacy of EU rules, (2) the greater the identification of the target government and society with the EU and (3) the higher 'domestic resonance' toward EU rules, the greater the likelihood of EU rule adoption will be (ibid. 2004: 667-668, 2005b: 18-20).

2.2 Empirical findings on (non)compliance with EU conditionality

In the subsequent paragraph the main empirical findings on (non)compliance with EU conditionality[16] will be discussed. In this way, potential gaps in research and starting points for future studies are identified.[17] Taking into account that the effectiveness of EU conditionality may differ across different issue areas and stages of the enlargement process (cf. Sedelmeier 2006: 6), it turns out to be useful to distinguish between 'democratic conditionality' and '*acquis* conditionality'.[18]

2.2.1 Compliance with democratic conditionality

Concerning democratic conditionality, domestic adoption costs and credible threats (exclusion, suspension of negotiations) and promises (association, membership) have been identified as the key variables for rule adoption (cf. Morlino/Magen 2009b: 253;

[15] See table 1 in the annex for an illustration of the overall theoretical model applied by Schimmelfennig and Sedelmeier (2005a).

[16] There are different ways to conceptualize the instrument of conditionality. 'Negative conditionality' is applied through non-military, yet coercive economic, political and diplomatic measures. By contrast, 'positive conditionality' rewards compliance with the provision of symbolic or material incentives.

[17] For reasons of scope and due to the particular focus on Croatia in the empirical part of this paper, I concentrate the following discussion of compliance with EU conditionality on those countries the EU officially offered the prospect of future membership. For an overview of empirical findings on the overall shape, effectiveness, and crucial mechanisms of EU 'rule transfer' via the ENP and beyond Europe see Börzel (2010), Gawrich et al. (2009), Jünemann/Knodt (2007), Magen et al. (2009), Nwobike (2005), Schimmelfennig (2009), Schimmelfennig/Scholtz (2008), Youngs (2001).

[18] 'Democratic conditionality' refers to the basic political foundations of the Union, such as human rights and liberal democracy, whereas 'acquis conditionality' concerns the concrete rules of the acquis communautaire. According to Schimmelfennig and Sedelmeier, the main incentive for compliance with democratic conditionality are, first, the setting up of institutional relations and, once this has been achieved, the opening of accession negotiations (cf. 2004: 669). As soon as concrete accession negotiations start, acquis conditionality sets in, i.e. compliance with the rules of the acquis communautaire is established as a precondition for further association. Consequently, the major external incentive for compliance with acquis conditionality is EU membership (cf. ibid. 2004: 669, 2005c: 212). Nonetheless, this distinction is rather conceptual since both acquis and democratic conditionality can overlap or alternate in being the most important mechanism (cf. ibid. 2005c: 212).

Schimmelfennig/Sedelmeier 2005c: 211; Youngs 2009).[19] By contrast, the inconsistent use of conditionality and the apparent lack of a determined timetable for future accession may decrease both incentives and credibility, which seems to have decelerated rule adoption in the WB (cf. Pridham 2007: 459; Sebastian 2008: 5-6; Vachudova 2005: 252).[20] The fact that certain conditions (such as compliance with minority rights and the Dayton Peace Accord, ICTY cooperation) are not part of the *acquis* may imply a lack of determinacy and legitimacy of EU conditionality. However, at least for the field of minority protection it was shown that it did not matter for compliance whether rules were also binding for EU member states, even though the EU's demands differed considerably between candidate states (e.g. Kelley 2004a; Schimmelfennig et al. 2003: 515; Schimmelfennig/Sedelmeier 2005c: 214-215; Schwellnus 2005).[21] Rather it appears that in the case of minority rights the gap in membership legislation could be offset by concrete demands in official EU documentations and the consistent way the member states insisted on full compliance as a precondition for membership (cf. Schimmelfennig 2005a: 119-121; for a more critical assessment see Sasse 2005).

Yet large material and symbolic benefits and high credibility alone do not provide for compliance with democratic conditionality. Rather, one has to take into account domestic adoption costs, too (cf. Ethier 2003: 117; Leeds 1999). In an analysis of the effects of membership incentives on compliance with EU conditionality in East and South East Europe, Schimmelfennig identified the party system as a crucial independent variable for external influence on domestic rule adoption (2005b: 855-857, 2007: 132-135).[22] In an "anti-liberal" party constellation adoption costs will be prohibitive, whereas in a "mixed" constellation liberal parties adopt democratic rules which raise the costs for subsequent anti-liberal coalitions to reverse course.[23] Regarding "liberal" party constellations, Schimmelfennig found that norm compliance depended on the issue area: if it was not contested, conditionality was unnecessary and the external actor could create a "virtuous circle" (cf. 2005b: 856, 2007: 133-

[19] For example, the approval of official candidate status in 1999 and the opening of accession negotiations in 2005 boosted the credibility of Turkey's membership promise. Apparently, that is why Turkey subsequently realized thorough human rights reforms (cf. Morlino/Magen 2009b: 229-232; Schimmelfennig 2005a: 121).

[20] Morlino and Magen found a similar nexus at work in of Romania, Serbia and the Ukraine (cf. 2009b: 229).

[21] It seems that in CEE the legitimacy of rules neither had a negative impact on the adoption of rules from the acquis. Neither the lack of EU competences vis-à-vis member states nor if member states ex post delayed access to the benefits or a patchy implementation record among the member states were found to have a negative impact on rule adoption, e.g., in the fields of free movement of people, administrative reform or social policy (cf. Schimmelfennig/Sedelmeier 2005c: 217-218). Nonetheless, such behavior apparently weakened the EU's and the member states' bargaining power which led to concessions toward the new member states (ibid.).

[22] The following argumentation is based on the assumption that – if political contestation and free elections are guaranteed – not only the incumbent government, but all major competitors will include external demands in their cost-benefit calculations since each of them may form part of a future government (cf. Schimmelfennig 2005b: 835, 2007: 132).

[23] The party constellation in Croatia was identified as "mixed" by Schimmelfennig (2007: 139; 2005b: 842).

134). However, if the norm was contested (e.g. in the case of minority issues in Latvia and Estonia), conditionality had to be applied and, at least in the case of CEE countries, ultimately proved successful (Schimmelfennig 2005b: 835-837, 2007: 133-134).

Similarly, if domestic veto players were confronted with low or negative costs, normative pressure and efficient assistance proved sufficient for rule adoption in 'low-politics' areas, e.g. rather technocratic reforms of the judicial system (cf. Morlino/Magen 2009b: 234). On the other hand, given moderate adoption costs, high incentives and credible conditionality proved to be sufficient for the EU to manipulate the target government's costs-benefits calculations in favor of rule adoption (cf. Schimmelfennig/Sedelmeier 2005c: 222). In autocratic and authoritarian states, however, thorough democratic reforms would imply exorbitant (power) costs to the incumbent regime.[24] Additionally, in more fragile democracies the EU might 'lock-in' democratic reforms: in times when reform-friendly liberal democratic forces form the government, EU rules are adopted which leaves subsequent authoritarian or populist governments with a *fait accompli* and implies extra-costs to revoke reforms (cf. Schimmelfennig/Sedelmeier 2005c: 222; Schimmelfennig 2007: 135). Yet it is contested whether such 'lock-in'-effects can be fully explained within purely rationalist argumentation, since it may have been due to persuasion or socialization effects that rather authoritarian forces preserved democratic rules and institutions once they reached power(cf. Börzel/Risse 2009: 15-16; Checkel 2005a: 809).[25]

Yet conditionality and external incentives can also work indirectly through the empowerment of domestic 'change agents' and the relative weakening of veto-players (cf. Morlino/Magen 2009: 31). Change agents or 'norm entrepreneurs', be they state or social actors, direct attention to democratic rules and, as a political strategy, change the way certain norms are perceived and talked about (cf. Finnemore/Sikking 1998: 897-899). This 'framing' aims at mobilizing public pressure in order to raise costs of reform-recalcitrant elites and redefines identities and interests of domestic decision-makers and the broader public via processes of persuasion and social learning (Johnson 2006).[26] In order to be successful, however, the public must be perceptive for ideas of democratic change in specific issue areas (or even ready to overthrow the regime) and the government/autocracy must not be

[24] Therefore, in countries like Slovakia, Bulgaria, Romania, Croatia or Serbia the EU's democratic conditionality turned out to be ineffective until democratic governments took over; a similar situation persists in Belarus today (cf. Schimmelfennig et al. 2003; Schimmelfennig/Sedelmeier 2004: 669-670, 2005c: 214; Rontoyanni/Korosteleva 2005; Vachudova 2005: 4, 98-104; Youngs 2009: 897).

[25] Also see Grabbe (2006: 202-203) on how socialization effects changed domestic actors' behavior in CEE.

[26] Snow et al. (1986) refer to this strategic activity as "frame alignment": "[b]y rendering events or occurrences meaningful, frames function to organize experience and guide action, whether individual or collective" (1986: 464). For the concept of 'strategic framing' see also Goffman (1974), Snow and Benford (1988).

sufficiently consolidated to suppress or marginalize democratic opposition (cf. Schimmelfennig/Sedelmeier 2005c: 214).[27]

To promote its external governance the EU sometimes also delegated command and control as well as consultancy tasks to other international organizations, e.g. to the OSCE in the WB (with regard to the setup of the Stability Pact in 1999).[28] Apart from that, there areb also cases of "parallel conditionality" (Schimmelfennig/Sedelmeier 2005b: 15) when the EU's leverage on domestic rule adoption is enhanced by other external actors, such as the US and NATO in the Balkans (cf. Schimmelfennig 2005: 22 for CEE).[29]

2.2.2 Compliance with *acquis* conditionality

In contrast to political conditions for membership, *acquis* conditionality does not directly affect the fundamental institutions of political power and therefore does not directly threaten the political survival of the target government. As concerns *acquis* conditionality, according to the empirical results of Schimmelfennig and Sedelmeier, a credible membership perspective and dependence of accession on (full) compliance with specific rules turned out as the key factors for rule adoption in CEE, whereas adoption costs and veto players mattered only with regard to the timing of rule adoption (cf. 2004: 673, 2005c: 210-211, 226; see also Hofer 2008: 175-180). As soon as *aquis* conditionality was applied in a certain issue area, formerly "patchy and selective" rule adoption has been detected to increase considerably, which is "a consistent feature across countries and issue areas" in CEE (Schimmelfennig/Sedelmeier 2005c: 215).[30] As has been found for CEE, once the membership perspective has become credible, the target government apparently rather considered the aggregate benefits of membership than the benefits in particular issue areas in its cost-benefit-calculations (cf. Schimmelfennig/Sedelmeier 2005c: 215-216). Therefore,

[27] In their study of 'hardship cases' (Romania, Serbia, Ukraine, Turkey), Morlino and Magen found that democratic conditionality was the least effective in those issue areas where relatively weak change agents encountered strong veto players whose power could only be challenged by external actors (2009b: 244-251).

[28] On the other hand, the OSCE often depended on the Union's democratic conditionality for its own leverage, e.g. when the OSCE successfully introduced many of its human rights goals into the Stabilization and Association Agreement (SAA) with Croatia (cf. Richter 2009b: 247-249; also see Vachudova 2005: 253 for the case of the ICTY). Therefore, analyzing the OSCE's effectiveness in rule extension (Richter 2009b) helps to illustrate EU conditionality and socialization mechanisms as the OSCE is not able to impose conditionality via hierarchical modes of governance for the lack of resources and power. Yet the OSCE might be more trustworthy among locals for the perceived lesser degree of politicization and the better crisis management compared to the EU in the 1990s which might be conducive for socialization processes and thus favour EU 'rule extension' (for the case of Serbia see Dallara 2009: 185).

[29] For example, in Serbia the EU referred to the OSCE and the Council of Europe when proposing its democratic conditionality policies in order to raise the legitimacy of its rules and consequently to enhance compliance. For an illustration of this mechanism regarding the issue of domestic war crimes trials see Commission (2004: 13).

[30] Additionally, if the EU clearly pointed out the salience of several issue areas toward the CEE countries, EU conditionality became more credible and hence rule adoption increased (cf. Treib/Falkner 2008: 161-164).

Schimmelfennig and Sedelmeier argue that in this case domestic power costs and the domestic veto player structure will rather delay than impede rule adoption while no systematic effect on the likelihood of rule adoption could be identified (cf. 2005c: 216). Another important domestic variable is the institutional and administrative capacity as the government might simply lack the resources to effectively manage and coordinate large bureaucracies or to sufficiently command (and/or socialize) veto-players within the state apparatus which will affect especially rule implementation.[31]

External incentives, however, fall short to explain instances of rule adoption when external incentives were low or absent (cf. Grabbe 2006: 201; Schimmelfennig/Sedelmeier 2005c: 220).[32] Moreover, during the transition, domestic reformers both in the CEE and in the Balkans have been looking for external templates for the modification or invention of domestic rules (cf. Grabbe 2001: 1014).[33] However, little knowledge exists about which factors facilitate or obstruct the internal and/or external diffusion of European ideas: "[l]*esson-drawing and/or mimicry* is probably the least researched area [...] with regard to Europeanization" [emphasis in the original] (Börzel/Risse 2009: 13). Incentive-based strategies aim at modifying behavior which makes them effective when it comes to the imposition of institutions and formal adoption of norms. Thereby they help to lock-in domestic reforms. However, mere conditionality policies are unable to cause genuine implementation and internalization of norms ('real change') and may even provoke counterproductive effects, when monitoring and the threat to be punished crowd out integrity and intrinsic motivation (cf. Morlino/Magen 2009b: 255; Richter 2009b: 111; Schimmelfennig 2005b: 831).[34] A similar point is made with regard to a possible subsequent slowdown of compliance and implementation or outright reversal of norms once states have

[31] See Elbasani 2009; Hille/Knill 2006; Treib/Falkner 2008: 165-168; Morlino/Magen 2009b: 250-251; Noutcheva/Bechev 2008; Richter 2009b: 379).

[32] As Schimmelfennig and Sedelmeier have found, countries like Slovenia, the Czech Republic, Hungary or Poland initiated both democratic and socio-economic reforms by their own initiative which implies that neither democratic nor acquis conditionality are necessary for rule adoption (cf. 2005c: 214, 218).

[33] Constructivist concepts of, on the one hand, normative rationality such as 'mimicry', 'symbolic imitation' and 'isomorphism' (Bikhchandani et al. 1998; DiMaggio/Powell 1991; Havemann 1993; Meyer/Rowan 1977; Polillo/Guillén 2005) or 'social learning' (Schimmelfennig/Sedelmeier 2004: 667-668, 2005b: 18-20), and, on the other hand, instrumental rationality such as 'lesson-drawing' (ibid. 2004: 668, 2005b: 22-25) or 'deliberate emulation' (Lavenex/Uçarer 2004; on 'modes of emulation' also see Jacoby 2004: 5-8) provide valuable insights why (and which) specific rules are chosen from a broader international compendium (cf. Jacoby 2004: 233-237; Schimmelfennig/Sedelmeier 2005c: 219). Moreover, they also outline the EU's "enabling impact" when domestic actors refer to the Union to legitimize their own political agenda (Diez et al. 2006: 573, 578-579). Thus, mechanisms of institutional isomorphism, policy transfer or policy diffusion may explain whether or not (and which) EU rules will be chosen (for an overview see Holzinger et al. 2007).

[34] In line with this, "[c]onsiderable evidence" has been found that state actors formally adopted rules while at the same time they obstructed implementation through the introduction of special amendments or the use of political interference and personal sabotage (cf. Grabbe 2006: 200-201; Morlino/Magen 2009b: 241-243; for the case of Croatia see Richter 2009a: 18).

gained membership status (cf. Falkner/Treib 2008; Grabbe 2006: 204; Schimmelfennig/Sedelmeier 2004: 676; Treib/Falkner 2008: 165).[35] However, recent findings of enduring compliance among new member states after their accession with both *acquis* and less formalized EU rules challenge the fundamental role of conditionality for compliance that dominates the rational choice literature (Epstein 2008b; Falkner/Treiber 2008; Pridham 2008; Schimmelfennig/Trauner 2009). Rather, it seems that strategic bargaining mechanisms must be accompanied and complemented by other means of socialization such as shaming and normative suasion to promote domestic change and provide for long-term democratization effects (see Checkel 2001: 563, 2005: 803; Kelley 2004b; Richter 2009b: 97, 106; Schimmelfennig 2003: 281-287).[36]

---

[35] See Subotić (2009: 364-365) who, going beyond the case of EU foreign policy, similarly holds that once external pressure is lifted compliance in the field of international justice will remain incomplete – no matter if target states are prone to conditionality or to "symbolic international pressure".

[36] For an analysis of the synthesis of rationalism and constructivism and a discussion on how a conjunction could generate valuable new theoretical insights and empirical results see Epstein (2008a), Fearon and Wendt (2005), Jacoby (2004: 20-40), Jupille et al. (2003), Ruggie (1998), Zürn and Checkel (2005), Wendt (1999).

3. Methodology and research design

The research design is a "within-case-analysis" of a "focused" and "structured" (George/Bennett 2005: 67) single case study that applies process-tracing to systematically place politics in the temporal context (Pierson 2004). As the aim of any research is "to make valid descriptive and causal inferences" (King et al. 1994: 3) I will adhere to the authors' advice to separate the research process into four elements: "the *research question*, the *theory*, the *data*, and the *use of the data*" [emphasis in the original] (King et al. 1994: 13). Besides, whether qualitative or quantitative, scientific research is valuable as long as it meets four criteria: "(1) [t]he goal is inference", (2) "the procedures are public", (3) "the conclusions are uncertain" and (4) "the content is the method" [in bold letters in the original] (King et al.1994: 7-9). The last decade in political science has brought about what Bennett and Elman (2006: 455) label a "renaissance in qualitative methods", while ultimately "researchers invariably face a choice between knowing more about less, or less about more" (Gerring 2007: 49).[37] Case studies are regarded as "valuable in testing hypotheses and particularly useful for theory development" as well as being effective in "achieving high conceptual validity" (George/Bennett 2005: 4). As Pevehouse (2005: 11) contests, there is a "dearth of research on the link between international organizations and democracy". Moreover, no meta-theory about EU enlargement or international democratization has been developed yet (cf. Richter 2009: 28). Furthermore, the number of countries which are subject to ICTY-related conditionality is very limited and the cases are highly complex. Finally, cases of reversal resistance and failure of EU conditionality have been mostly excluded from theoretically informed research, so there still is little in-depth knowledge about crucial factors and variables that hinder or enable EU 'rule extension' to third countries (cf. Elbasani 2009: 5; Magen/Morlino 2009: 13). Therefore, notwithstanding the shortcomings of single case studies (cf. Pierson 2004: 139-142) a case study approach is suitable for this particular research purpose to (potentially) uncover causal mechanisms which might be at work in other comparable cases as well (cf. Georg/Bennett 2005: 114-115; Bennett/Elman 2006: 462).[38] The case of Croatia is particularly worth of scrutiny as despite favorable conditions in light of the democratization process and swift EU association after 2000, EU 'rule extension' in the war crimes issue turned out to be only partially successful.

[37] For a discussion of advantages and disadvantages of case studies see Gerring (2007: 37-63) and Yin (2009).

[38] Apparently, particular qualitative and quantitative methods may differ substantially. However, the "same logic of inference" applies to both (King et al. 1994: 3) and "[t]he product of a good case study is insight" (Gerring 2007: 7).

The research design is "structured" since the investigation of identical, carefully selected variables is standardized, and, besides, it is "focused" on a specific research objective (George/Bennett 2005: 67), namely variation in Croatia's compliance with EU rules on ICTY cooperation. Moreover, as I already stressed in the introduction, the EIM complemented by the 'external governance approach' provides the "theoretical focus appropriate for that objective" (ibid.). Yet to demonstrate that hypothesized causal mechanisms[39] were at work between the independent variable (systems of EU rules) and the outcome of the dependent variable (compliance with EU rules) it is necessary to identify "the intervening causal process – the causal chain and causal mechanism" (George/Bennett 2005: 206-207; cf. Bennett/Elman 2006: 459). A promising method to uncover "a series of theoretically predicted intermediate steps" (Checkel 2005b: 5) is process-tracing which, "if done properly, [...] places theory and data in close proximity" (Checkel 2005b: 22).[40] Moreover, examining ICTY-related EU conditionality in Croatia fulfills two basic methodological conditions. Firstly, a question should be raised "*which is 'important' in the real world*" [emphasis in the original] (King et al. 1994: 15; cf. George/Bennett 2005: 69). Secondly, the study should increase scientific knowledge in a particular scholarly literature (ibid.). Data to trace these processes within the case study comprise primary sources, media reports and secondary literature that largely remains descriptive to provide for a transparent and comprehensible research process.

[39] According to Schelling (1998: 32-33), a 'social mechanism' is a "set of plausible hypotheses that could be the explanation for some social phenomenon, the explanation being in terms of interactions between individuals and other individuals, or between individuals and some social aggregate".

[40] Nonetheless, next to the empirical insights gained from process-tracing and the possibility to combine it with other methods, it entails many potential risks and disadvantages, such as the subjectivity of the author (cf. Richter 2009b: 47, 83) or its limited contributions to theory-building (see Bennett/Elman 2006, 2007; Checkel 2005b: 17-21; Gerring 2007: 172-185; King et al. 1994: 85-87, 225-228).

4. Empirical analysis

4. 1 The role of ICTY conditionality within the EU enlargement framework

Although the Copenhagen criteria for EU accession were outlined already in 1993, only with the *Avis* in 1997 did the EU start to apply these conditionality principles, while the Luxemburg European Council (December 1997) simultaneously introduced three new key operative elements to its enhanced pre-accession strategy, namely Accession Partnerships, annual assessment through progress reports and accession-driven economic assistance.[41] At this time, democratic consolidation in CEE (except Slovakia) was basically completed that is why the EU's democratic conditionality in the 1990s was focused on democratic consolidation rather than democratic transition (cf. Pridham 2007: 449).[42] Nonetheless, due to the specific legacy of warfare and ethnic conflict in the region, the EU in 1997 extended the conditionality framework to be applied toward the WB countries by state-building issues, namely by the obligation to fully comply with the Dayton Peace Agreement (1995) and the UNSC Resolution 1244 on Kosovo (1999), to fully cooperate with the ICTY and to enable refugee return.[43] Importantly, the 1997 guidelines introduced a gradual and bilateral approach, within which different degrees of conditionality would be applied in the fields of financial assistance, trade preferences, economic cooperation and the establishment of contractual relations (European Council 1997).[44] In June 2000, at the Feira European Council, all WB countries (except Serbia) obtained the status 'potential candidate'.[45] At the Zagreb Summit (November 2000), the Stabilization and Association Process (SAP) was institutionalized which became the overall framework for the WB countries "all the way to their future

[41] The 1993 Copenhagen criteria made EU accession dependent upon achieving "stability of institutions guaranteeing democracy, the rule of law, human rights and respect for and protection of minorities, the existence of a functioning market economy as well as the capacity to cope with competitive pressure and market forces within the Union [...] [and the] Union's capacity to absorb new members [...]" (European Council 1993: 13).

[42] With the entry into force of the Amsterdam Treaty (1997) on May 1999, the political conditions for membership were institutionalized. Art. 6(1) states that the EU is "founded on the principles of liberty, democracy, respect for human rights and fundamental freedoms, and the rule of law, principles which are common to the Member States" (Art. 6). Any European state that accepts these principles may apply to become a member state (Art. 49).

[43] See European Council (1997) for a list of the conditions to be fulfilled by the WB countries.

[44] The 1997 criteria also became the conditionality framework of the EU's Regional Approach of 1996 which set out the guidelines for the EU's uniform approach to the WB countries (European Council 1996). Moreover, on 17 May 1999, amid NATO's ongoing air campaign against Serbia, the EU foreign ministers launched the Stability Pact with similar entry requirements and conditionality policies as with regard to the Regional Approach (European Council 1999).

[45] For an overview of the current stage of accession negotiations of the individual WB countries see table 2 in the annex.

accession" (European Council 2003: 13).[46] At the joint EU-Balkans summit in Thessaloniki (June 2003) the SAP was deepened through the establishment of European Partnerships and the unequivocal statement that "the future of the Balkans is within the EU" (Council of the European Union 2003: Annex A).[47] The SAP is made up of exceptional trade measures, financial assistance and, most importantly, the Stabilization and Association Agreement (SAA).[48] The principle of democratic conditionality of reward was explicitly integrated both in the CARDS (Art. 5) and the IPA (Art. 21) Council Regulations on financial assistance which has enabled the EU to suspend project funding in case of non-compliance with its rules (Council of the European Union 2000, 2006).[49] In the light of a perceived "enlargement fatigue", the experiences of the latest enlargement rounds and the difficult task of enlargement in the WB ahead, the EU in December 2004 introduced new instruments to enlargement politics and tightened its conditionality approach.[50] Regarding democratic conditionality, the Council, acting by qualified majority, "in case of a serious and persistent breach" of democratic principles received the right to suspend accession negotiations and lay down the conditions for resumption (European Council 2004c: point I.8.23).[51]

4.2 The case of Croatia

Compliance with ICTY-related conditionality comprises many different subfields such as the arrest and transfer of indictees to The Hague, access to documents, witness protection or domestic war crimes trials. However, owing to the size restriction of this paper, I shall limit the analysis to the most important field, namely the transfer of indictees to the ICTY. The

---

[46] Besides, it was announced that during the accession process each state will be evaluated by its own progress, thereby introducing the so-called principle of 'each-by-its-own-merits' (see Vachudova 2005: 112-120). At the Feira European Council (June 2000) the EU for the first time explicitly distanced itself from the uniform approach and set up differentiated recommendations for each of the WB states (cf. European Council 2000).

[47] The European Partnerships – that were modeled on the Accession Partnerships of CEE – identified different priorities for every WB country which are to be met within a short term (12-24 months) and medium term (3 to 4 years).

[48] All WB countries except Serbia were eligible to receive funds from the OBNOVA (1996-2000) and PHARE programs until 5 December 2000 when they were replaced by CARDS. On 1 January 2007, the IPA (Instrument for Pre-Accession Assistance) was introduced to streamline the EU's financial allocations and to substitute for CARDS, PHARE, ISPA and SAPARD. Besides, as an additional incentive to comply with EU rules, a clear differentiation between 'potential candidate' and 'candidate' countries was introduced qualifying the latter for additional IPA-funds which in total sum up to almost €11.5 billion for the period between 2007 and 2013 (Council of the European Union 2006b).

[49] Thereby, the EU established "one of the most comprehensive conditionality clauses ever embodied in a Community legal instrument regulating external assistance" (Pippan 2004: 232).

[50] Since then, once accession negotiations start, the acquis is broken down into specific chapters while the Council may lay down benchmarks for the suspension or (re)opening of each chapter. Moreover, permanent 'safeguard clauses' can be introduced. See European Council (2004: point I.8.23) for the new framework of enlargement negotiations. The tightened democratic conditionality approach has been reiterated and specified in the subsequent enlargement strategies (see Commission 2005a: 3, 2006: 5-7).

[51] See Fierro (2003), Pippan (2004), Pridham (2007) and Sjursen/Smith (2003) for a detailed discussion of both the application and the content of EU conditionality.

case study will focus on the three key indictments to illustrate the main factors which favored Croatia's (non)compliance with ICTY conditionality: that of Mirko Norac, the one of general Bobetko and the Gotovina case.

4.2.1 Introduction: the political context in Croatia

Croatia from 1995 until 2000 might be labeled a "hybrid regime" or as "corrupt populist pluralism" (Ramet 2008: 157) due to its bad record on civil and freedom rights, strong control of the media, an extensive patronage-based network and disrespect for parliamentary institutions (cf. Bartlett 2003: 49-55; BTI 2003: 2; Richter 2009b: 231).[52] Moreover, at the end of the 1990s, Croatia was largely isolated because of the regime's disregard for international norms (NYT 1999, 2000c).[53] What is more, Tuđman's restrictive policies led to sanctions by the International Monetary Fund (IMF), the exclusion from EU assistance under the PHARE program and from NATO's Partnership for Peace program (PfP) (cf. BTI 2003: 1-3) which exacerbated the economic and social situation and thus was one important factor for the defeat of Tuđman's HDZ (Croatian Democratic Union) in the 2000 elections which until then had dominated the political system (cf. Richer 2009b: 215; Zakošek 2008: 601).[54] Moreover, Tuđman only very reluctantly and sporadically cooperated with the ICTY, especially with regard to the military operations 'Flash' and 'Storm' (cf. AFP 2001; BBC 1999; Del Ponte 2008: 315-321; Mundis 2001).[55] In order to prevent democratic reforms and to legitimize his policies, the Tuđman regime built on historical nationalist ideas.[56] After 1992, new parties emerged next to the dominant HDZ and, after 2000, the fragmentation of existing parties and the foundation of several new ones resulted in the transformation into a multiparty system (cf. Richter 2009b: 220; Zakošek 2008: 600).

---

[52] On Croatia under Tuđman see Kusovac (2000) and Uzelak (1997).

[53] For an overview of the EU's policies toward former Yugoslavia and its successor states as well as the domestic situation in the respective countries from 1991-2001, see Blockmans (2007: 111-175) and ICG(2001a). For an excellent discussion of the scientific literature on the causes and consequences of the breakup of former Yugoslavia, see Ramet (2005).

[54] Prior to the democratic regime change, the domestic governing elites in Croatia (as well as in Serbia) had not been susceptible to EU rules and conditionality that is why the EU tried to increase its limited leverage by supporting the respective democratic opposition groups (cf. Vachudova 2005: 253).

[55] Both in 1996 and in 1999, the then ICTY presidents officially reported Croatia's noncompliance with the tribunal and obstruction to its investigations to the UNSC (UNSC 1996, 1999).The 1996 complaint centered on Croatia's failure to arrest and hand over Ivica Rajić, while in 1999 the then tribunal president focused on noncompliance with the indictment for Mladen Naletilić (ibid.).

[56] During the 1990s, the powerful narrative of the so-called 'Homeland War' was created to stress the purely 'defensive' character of the recapture of Croatian soil seized by Serbian forces in the 1990s and to glorify the Croatian nation and its 'war heroes' while references to nationalist historical symbols continue to be used in the political discourse, including the glorification of fascist Ustaša-regime (cf. Goldstein 1999; Radonic 2007; Zakošek 2007; Žanić 2005, 2007).

After Tuđman's death in December 1999, early elections were called in January 2000.[57] A broad majority center-left coalition government of six opposition parties (*Šestorka)*, led by the Social Democratic Party of Croatia (SDP) took over and elected the reformed communist Ivica Račan (SDP) as prime minister.[58] One month later, Stjepan Mesić won the presidential elections, a pro-Western reformer with an unambiguous anti-nationalist stance (cf. Richter 2009b: 218).[59] With the approval of president Mesić, Croatia's political system was subsequently converted from a presidential into a parliamentary system (cf. Ramet 2008: 210).[60] During the election campaign the opposition movement, led by the Social Liberal leader, Dražen Budiša, and by the Social Democratic leader, Ivica Račan, promised to break with Tuđman's authoritarian legacy, to (re)integrate Croatia into the Western community and to cooperate with the ICTY (cf. BTI 2003: 2; NYT 1999, 2000a, 2000b).[61]

Strong national identity conflicts persist in present-day Croatia: on the one hand, the democratic reforms have constantly enjoyed high legitimacy among the population and since 2002 at the latest there has been a broad consensus toward European integration and democratic values in Croatia (cf. Richter 2009a: 17, 2009b: 216). Nonetheless, nationalist feelings and the political will to defend the independent Croat state (*Državotvornost*) have remained strong, both among political elites and the broader public.[62]

4.2.2 Phase I: the Račan government (2000-2003)

The EU and the US immediately acclaimed the opposition's victory. Moreover, they pledged a rapid increase of financial aid as well as future integration into EU and NATO structures – under the condition of full ICTY cooperation (cf. NYT 2000d). Yet the Račan government was soon given an initial foretaste of the difficult task of bringing in line domestic and external demands. The unexpectedly harsh sentence of 45 years imposed on general Blaškić by the ICTY in March 2000 led to widespread anger in Croatia and to public demonstrations while it also undermined the tribunal's reputation among state officials (cf. Bartlett 2003: 80;

[57] Importantly, both Tuđman (on 10 December 1999) and his defense minister Gojko Šušak (in May 1998) died without being indicted by the Hague tribunal.

[58] See table 3 in the annex for the turnout of the 2000 parliamentary elections.

[59] To protest Tuđman's aggressive policies towards Bosnia, in 1994 Mesić had left the HDZ and, together with Josip Manolić, founded a new opposition party – the Independent Croatian Democrats (HND) (cf. Ramet 2008: 209). He was elected by 56% in the final round of the presidential elections (cf. Bartlett 2003:58; NYT 2000e).

[60] In terms of ICTY cooperation, since the constitutional amendments were adopted in 2000 and 2001, the president has only very little decision-making authority (cf. Peskin/Boduszyński 2003: 1132).

[61] Budiša, the leader of the Croatian Social Liberal Party (HSLS), in the communist era was a prominent nationalist dissident. Thus, he added nationalist credibility to the coalition government that Račan's SDP as a party of reformed communists would not be able to develop (cf. ICG 2001b: 4).

[62] For a more detailed analysis of the role of identity issues in Croatian politics see Brkljačić (2003), Jansen (2002), Madunić (2009), Renner/Horelt (2008), Tull (2003: 132), UNDP (2006: 157-158), Zakošek (2008: 598).

ICG 2001b: 3).[63] What is more, the coalition government was confronted with a heavy burden of massive economic and financial problems and weakened by the differing ideologies and constituencies of the ruling parties, leaving little room for political maneuver (cf. Bicanic/Franicevic 2003: 16-22; BTI 2003; NYT 2000c). Nonetheless, one of the first official acts of the new Račan government was a declaration on cooperation with the ICTY on 14 April 2000 in which Račan stated that "[e]ither Croatia brings these criminals to justice or it is not a state of law" (cited in Massari 2005: 266).[64] The extradition of two indictees to The Hague as the first – yet very cautious – move of cooperation was immediately rewarded with acceptance for NATO's PfP program by 25 May 2000 (cf. Bartlett 2003: 83).[65] Apparently, keeping in mind that the tribunal president had already credibly threatened Croatia with sanctions before (UNSC 1999) and factoring into its calculations the huge benefits of approaching EU and NATO compared to rather low costs,[66] the Croatian government eventually handed over Naletilić while it had delayed his extradition before and thus ultimately complied with EU conditionality (cf. Peskin//Boduszyński 2003: 1125).

The EU, on the other hand, was very eager to use the 'window of opportunity' provided by the regime change and thus, in May 2000, adopted a Feasibility Study for a SAA which praised Croatia's "major steps" regarding ICTY cooperation (Commission 2000: 7), citing Croatia's declaration on cooperation with the ICTY from 14 April 2000 in which it acknowledged the tribunal's jurisdiction on the 'Storm' and 'Flash' military operations and promised to step up ICTY cooperation. However, it was not external incentives alone that tempted the government to reconsider its relatively tentative approach: the murder of Milan Levar – a Croatian key witness to the ICTY regarding the atrocities committed in the Gospić area – in August 2000 clearly illustrated the need to take a more proactive stance to safeguard public order and security. Thus, the government decided to intensify its efforts against alleged war criminals, yet – keeping in mind potential public turmoil – it called for future trials to be held in Croatia instead of The Hague in order not to involve the ICTY (cf. Bartlett 2003: 81-

[63] However, although it had been the heaviest penalty imposed by the tribunal so far, a majority of Croats still backed ICTY cooperation (cf. Peskin/Boduszyński 2003: 1125). Blaškić as the commander of the Croat paramilitary forces in Bosnia was neither a member of the regular Croatian army nor directly linked to the 'Homeland War' that was fought in Croatia – a fact that in general made it much less sensitive to hand over Bosnian Croats than Croatian generals (cf. ibid.: 1124).

[64] In protest against the declaration, the HDZ's members of the Sabor walked out of the parliament hall during the vote and took part in street manifestations among war veterans and other right wing politicians (cf. BBC 2000; Central Europe Review 2000a).

[65] Regarding NATO integration, the Račan government profited from Croatia's cooperation over NATO's air campaign against the Federal Republic of Yugoslavia (FRY) in 1999 and that Račan was able to capitalize on the extradition of the indicted Bosnian Croats Vinko Martinović and Mladen Naletilić to The Hague who had been transferred in August 1999 and in March 2000 respectively (cf. Bartlett 2003: 80-81; ICG 2001b: 3).

[66] Already the Tuđman government had decided to extradite Naletilić (cf. Bartlett 2003: 80-81).

82).[67] Consequently, in September 2000 the government arrested two generals and ten other police and army officers for charges linked to the Gospić atrocities and other crimes, irrespective of the outrage it provoked among nationalists and HDZ supporters (cf. ibid.: 81-82). Besides, president Mesić took a decisive stance against a potential military coup when he dismissed Mirko Norac and seven other generals who were still serving in the army by then after they had written a public letter of protest against ICTY cooperation; remarkably, his action was met with "widespread public approval" (ICG 2001b: 8; see also Central Europe Review 2000b). On the other hand, in October 2000 the Croatian parliament passed the "Declaration on the Patriotic War" which presented the war in Croatia as purely defensive and legitimate, whereas crimes committed by Croat forces were systematically denied (cf. Cruvellier/Valiñas 2006: 3).[68] Notwithstanding the tribunal's renewed criticism in the second half of 2000 in view of restricted access to documents and key figures (cf. UNSC 2001: 25, 35),[69] overall compliance was deemed satisfactory by the EU. Consequently, negotiations for a SAA with Croatia were announced at the EU summit in Zagreb on 24 November 2000.

Nonetheless, the ever more tense relationship with the nationalists escalated and precipitated a serious political crisis when, on 7 February 2001, the local Rijeka court issued an arrest warrant for retired general Mirko Norac for his alleged involvement in the aforementioned Gospić killings. Following Norac's indictment – an acclaimed war hero among Croatian nationalists and the first high-ranking Croatian officer to face war crimes investigations – Croatia's main road was blocked for five days and mass rallies were organized throughout the country while Norac went into hiding (cf. BBC 2001a, 2001b).[70] In response, Račan and his minister of interior declared the government would not give in to the right-wing mobilization that would, domestically, put Croatia's democratic stability and legal order at risk, ignore the constitutional separation of powers by not showing due respect to the judiciary, harm the economy and, internationally, bring the country to the brink of sanctions

[67] To that effect, by October 2003, Račan authorized four local courts to try supposed war criminals (cf. Commission 2004b: 31), whereas the EU criticized that they "do not function" and that past experience with local war crimes trials in Croatia "leaves a lot to desire" (Commission 2004b: 31, 2005: 25).

[68] The Declaration claims that "the Republic of Croatia led a just and legitimate, defensive and liberating, and not aggressive and occupational war against anyone, in which she defended its territory from the great Serbian aggressor within its internationally recognized borders" (cited in UNDP 2006: 154). Moreover, article 5 of the Declaration asks the state to "provide full protection, respect and welfare" of all the "defenders" (cited in Jovic 2009: 20).

[69] Apart from that, Goran Granić, Croatia's deputy prime minister, had stressed Croatia's readiness to withdraw cooperation even at the prize of damaging its international reputation if the tribunal would not end its "politicized" working approach (cited in ICG 2001b: 3).

[70] The anti-government protests that have been a long time in preparation culminated on 11 February 2000 when more than 100,000 people gathered in Split for a demonstration under the slogan "We are all Mirco Norac", while they condemned any cooperation with the ICTY and demanded the reformist centre-left coalition to step down for betraying the 'Homeland War' (cf. NYT 2001a).

and isolation (cf. BBC 2001a; NYT 2001a). President Mesić blamed the nationalist opposition of coordinating the civil unrest while using the veterans for their selfish motive to regain power, adding that Norac had to surrender to the court for the charges related to the killing of civilians no matter his merits in the defense of Gospić (cf. BBC 2001a, 2001b). Thus, in view of the widespread resentment[71] against trying the lauded 'wartime heroes' government officials framed the issue of justice for war crimes as an important cornerstone for establishing democracy and the rule of law, while ICTY cooperation was justified in the name of Croatia's European identity.[72] To calm tensions and to unify the shaky coalition government, Račan and Mesić met in a face to face talk with Norac who declared his readiness to turn himself in provided that he would not be tried in The Hague (cf. Central Europe Review 2001). Apparently, the breakthrough was made when the ICTY publicly declared it did not intend to seek his extradition (ICTY 2001a). Both ICTY and EU officials exerted only moderate pressure, presumably because they did not want to unnecessarily undermine the democratic forces within the county taking into account the more sensitive cases to come. Shortly after, the general surrendered to the Croatian police. Yet although the government scored a political success when the SAA was initialed in May 2001 (cf. ICG 2001b: 1), in the same month the six-party coalition was weakened in the wake of local elections that were held on 20 May 2001.[73] Furthermore, following the transfer of Milošević to The Hague on 28 June 2001, the ICTY decided it would now be appropriate to give up its relative leniency toward Croatia and consequently exerted more pressure on the Račan government. After the ICTY's chief prosecutor, Carla Del Ponte, had informed the government already in June 2001 (cf. Del Ponte 2008: 328), in early July the sealed indictments for two high-ranking Croatian generals became public. They asked for the arrest and transfer of Rahim Ademi[74] who still served in the army by then and famed Ante Gotovina,

[71] 71 According to a survey conducted by the Croatian newspaper Slobodna Dalmacija, 66% of the respondents objected Norac's extradition to the Tribunal. On the other hand, 46% of those interviewed stated they were in favor of putting him on trial in Croatia in case of sufficient prove of his responsibility for war crimes, whereas 31% stated that since he had won credit as a soldier he should be exempted from any legal prosecution (all numbers cited in Peskin/Boduszyński 2003: 1140).

[72] By contrast, Ivo Sanader, who in 2003 would lead the HDZ back to power, aimed to revive the party's former strength when he blatantly threatened the Račan government with public turmoil in case it would not end ICTY cooperation and resign voluntarily (cf. NYT 2001a). However, he rather did so due to political opportunism than out of personal nationalist conviction as he needed to win the internal strife against the radical right-wing hardliners within the fragmented HDZ to prepare the ground for the HDZ's transformation into a more moderate conservative party modeled on the Western European Christian democratic parties (cf.ICG 2001b: 9).

[73] Following the elections, the regional Istrian Democratic Assembly (IDS) quit the national government, while Budiša's HSLS suffered from a very poor overall result, getting not enough votes even to enter the assembly in Zagreb (cf. ICG 2001b: 4-5). The Croatian Peasant Party (HSS), however, performed strongly in the countryside and thus complemented the SDP's positive turnout in urban areas (cf. ibid.: 9).

[74] Rahim Ademi – together with Janko Bobetko and Mirko Norac – was charged for the alleged atrocities committed against Serb inhabitants in the Međak Pocket in September 1993. For the ICTY case information

the commander of operation 'Storm' (*Oluja*), Croatia's final army offensive in August 1995 that was launched to reclaim Serb-held Krajina and that was regarded by the Croatian public as the final act in the country's painful war of liberation that led to today's independent state.[75] Thus, indictments were no longer issued only for Bosnian Croats who committed crimes in Bosnia, but for key figures of the 'Homeland War'.

Even though the February crisis could be diffused with a compromise, it appeared that the Račan government in the wake of the Norac indictment had come to realize that in case of cooperating too closely with the Tribunal it would deteriorate its popular support, potentially fall victim to the whims of the opposition exploiting the issue, or even jeopardize its political survival (cf. Pavlaković 2008: 455). Consequently, it had to take a cautious approach bringing in line its own interests with EU conditionality and demands of the international community. Following an emergency session of his cabinet, Račan declared his government would be ready to arrest and extradite any suspects charged by the tribunal (cf. UN Wire 2001).[76] The cabinet decision, however, came at a high cost as it led to the immediate resignation of four ministers, all of whom were members of the Social Liberal Party (HSLS), the second largest party in the coalition.[77] In response, domestic politics took center stage when Račan called a vote of confidence on 15 July 2001 (cf. CNN 2001a) from which he emerged strengthened as he won it decisively.[78] Remarkably, in his speech to parliament Račan made clear that he did not support the indictments and that compliance with the tribunal's demands was a painful necessity and thus a matter of political rationality.[79] Apparently as a strategy to appease the

---

sheet on the 'Međak Pocket' case (IT-04-78) linked to Norac and Ademi see http://www.icty.org/x/cases/norac/cis/en/cis-ademinorac.pdf (accessed on 11 August 2013). For the initial Ademi indictment as of 21 May 2001 see http://www.icty.org/x/cases/ademi/ind/en/ade-ii010608e.htm (accessed on 11 August 2013).

[75] Gotovina, among other things, was indicted of ordering the unlawful killing of at least 150 ethnic Serbs and expelling about 150,000 more during operation "Storm" between 4 August and 15 November 1995 (ICTY 2001b). Regarding the aforesaid operation, on 14 July 2006 the ICTY built a joint "Gotovina et al." case (IT-06-90), including charges against Mladen Markač and Ivan Čermak whose indictments were issued on 24 February 2004.
For the ICTY case information sheet see http://www.icty.org/x/cases/gotovina/cis/en/cis_gotovina_al_en.pdf (accessed on 11 August 2013). For the text of the initial Gotovina indictment as of 21 May 2001 see http://www.icty.org/x/cases/gotovina/ind/en/gotii010608e.htm (accessed on 11 August 2013).

[76] Referring to Croatia's European identity and obviously trying to "use international constraints" (Grodsky 2009: 27), he stressed that refusing cooperation "would return us into the abyss of the troubled Balkans, from which even Serbia" was escaping (cited in UN Wire 2001), while he promised that Croatia "respects its international responsibilities no matter how painful it might be" to avoid that Croatia turned into "a Balkan dwarf and an international outcast" (cited in RFE/RL 2001b).

[77] The four cabinet members who retired were Goran Granić, deputy prime minister; Hrvoje Kraljević, the science and technology minister; Jozo Radoš, the defense minister; and Goranko Fižulić, the economy minister (cf. CNN 2001a).

[78] While the prime minister needed a simple majority of 76 votes, actually 93 out of the 151 parliamentarians voted in favor of the coalition government, 36 against it and 22 were absent (cf. RFE/RL 2001).

[79] In addition to that, he announced that "the government will do everything it can, through legal proceedings, to assist the defense of the suspects in relation to charges we cannot accept" (cited in RFE/RL 2001b).

right wing parties and veteran groups who threatened to use "the most radical measures" (UN Wire 2001), Račan also sent a letter to Del Ponte – the content became public shortly after – in which he adopted nationalist rhetoric and openly criticized the tribunal for several allegations, including that of forced deportation of about 150,000 Serbs in 1995 (cf. RFE/RL 2001b).[80] President Mesić also gave his backing of the cabinet decision.[81] Moreover, Mesić managed to take pressure off the coalition as he was able to convince Ademi to surrender voluntarily to The Hague, as announced by Račan on 9 July 2001 (cf. BBC 2001c; CNN 2001b). Ademi turned himself in on 25 July 2001 (cf. UNSC 2001: 34).[82]

Regarding Gotovina, however, the rhetorical commitments were not followed by any remarkable deeds. Even though Gotovina had, already in early July 2001, made it clear that he was not ready to surrender to The Hague, no serious actions for his arrest were taken by the government; in the end of the month it became obvious that the general had been tipped off and gone into hiding (cf. Peskin/Boduszyński 2003: 1130). Nonetheless, apparently Račan's pledge to cooperate fully on the ICTY indictments in addition to Ademi's surrender to The Hague were sufficient to satisfy the EU representatives by then, as no major points of critique have been raised in the following months. The fact that Gotovina was on the run, on the other hand, helped to temporarily ease the pressure exerted by nationalist groups and the voter bloc of moderate Croatians who represented a crucial voter bloc (cf. Grodsky 2009: 26) as they may have been in favor of the government's general policies, but suspicious of investigating the war period. Apart from that, the government was enabled to use 'strategic talk' (Schimmelfennig 2003: 194-228), i.e. to officially express its determination to arrest Gotovina highlighting at the same time the inability to do so as his whereabouts would be unknown.[83] Notwithstanding Račan's failure to intensify the search for Gotovina and launch serious measures against his support network, the government's incomplete compliance was not met

[80] Apart from that, he adopted the nationalists' accusations that ICTY indictments imposed collective guilt on the Croatian nation, when he challenged the tribunal for some parts of the Gotovina indictment that "appeared to criminalize the entire campaign" of operation Storm (cited in ICG 2001b: 5; see also Commission 2004b: 30).

[81] Mesić stated that "[t]he Croatian people must not and will not be hostage to those who bloodied their hands and brought shame on Croatia's name, no matter how deserving they might be in other respects" (cited in RFE/RL 2001a). In reference to the indictment that labeled operation Storm a "joint criminal enterprise" and thus implied the risk that the Croatian state itself might be criminalized (cf. Subotić 2009: 379), Mesić pointed out that the ICTY does not try "nations, but suspects" (cited in NYT 2001b).

[82] After the case had been transferred to Croatia in September 2005, Ademi was acquitted in May 2008. However, important witnesses refused to testify due to intimidations and threats (cf. Amnesty International 2009: 10-11).

[83] Del Ponte, however, in an address to the United Nations Security Council (UNSC) in October 2002 expressed her view that Gotovina had been "allowed to evade arrest", adding that he "is now enjoying a safe haven in the territory of Croatia" (ICTY 2002).

with significant pressure by the EU (Pavlaković 2008: 455-456). The SAA was signed on 29 October 2001 and ratified in Croatia on 5 December 2001.[84]

The indictment of Janko Bobetko

Yet Croatia's relations with the EU were strained when, in September 2002, the tribunal's explosive and extremely unpopular indictment for general Janko Bobetko, the 83-old former army chief of staff and national hero, was unsealed (cf. Pavlaković 2008: 456).[85] Anticipating high domestic political costs,[86] in contrast to July 2001, this time Račan did not wait for the nationalists to mobilize, but immediately portrayed himself as a sharp critic of the "unconstitutional" indictment that would intend to criminalize Croatia's war of independence (cited in Peskin/Boduszyński 2003: 1132). Apparently, he subscribed to the universal view among Croatian politicians as in the end of September 2002 the national parliament unanimously expressed its opposition to the indictment (ibid.).[87] Bobetko, on the other hand, was supported by a very vocal group of veto-players, including high-ranking members of the Croatian Catholic church who called on the population to "unite in the face of the external pressure" (The Guardian 2002) as well as veteran associations and elements within the security forces who expressed their readiness to use violence to frustrate his arrest; even "the threat of a coup was palpable" (Pavlaković 2008: 456-457).[88] Bobetko himself said he would rather die than turn himself in voluntarily (cf. NYT 2002a). Moreover, following the exit of the HSLS from the governing coalition in summer 2002 due to an ongoing border dispute with Slovenia, Račan's room for maneuver was further marginalized (cf. Altmann/Kasch 2002: 3; Peskin/Boduszyński 2003: 1133). The chances of the SDP to win the ballot in case of early elections were considered minimal as it was deemed difficult to find coalition partners

[84] In parallel to the signing procedure, the arrest warrant for Gotovina was forwarded to the competent local authorities (cf. Hartmann 2009: 69).

[85] Bobetko was charged with authorizing atrocities against Serbian civilians in the Međak Pocket in 1993. For the text of the initial indictment see http://www.icty.org/x/cases/bobetko/ind/en/bob-ii020826-e.pdf (accessed on 11 August 2013).

[86] According to a public opinion survey, in late September 2002 84% of the respondents were against Bobetko's transfer to The Hague, with 71% opposing it even if this meant that political and economic sanctions were to be imposed (cf. Peskin/Boduszyński 2003: 1133).

[87] The discrete critic Mesić was a notable exception, who, in his weekly address to the nation, condemned the "anti-European and anti-democratic" character of nationalist resistance against ICTY cooperation (cited in Subotić 2009: 377). By contrast, deputy prime minister Goran Granić sharply criticized Mesić's support of the indictment and accused him of undermining Croatia's bargaining power (cf. Altmann/Kasch 2002: 3).

[88] Račan as well as Sanader from 2003 onwards shied away from implementing lustration and replacing HDZ apparatchiks who thus continued to fill leadership positions within the intelligence apparatus, administration, military and judiciary and successfully obstructed the domestic implementation of EU rules, most notably in the legal and administrative fields (cf. Cruvellier/Valiñas 2006: 30-31; Ramet 2008: 211; Richter 2009a: 18-19; 2009b: 219, 223, 279, 289).

(cf. Altmann/Kasch 2002: 3).[89] Noncompliance, however, carried the risk of international sanctions and isolation and thus the loss of the badly needed financial resources, while the opposition would seek to capitalize on the government's deteriorated international standing (cf. ibid.: 7). Thus, Račan attempted to buy time while portraying himself as cooperative: to delay Bobetkos's handover, Račan stressed the general's critical state of health. The stalling tactic ultimately turned out to be successful when, in early February 2003, the tribunal's doctors declared that Bobetko was medically unfit to stand trial (cf. NYT 2002b, 2003a). Although the indictment remained in place, the general got away unpunished with his death on 29 April 2003.

Initially, the EU in the Bobetko case exerted rather moderate pressure and pursued a rather inconsistent agenda, thus diluting the conditionality principle.[90] For example, in September 2002, the EU foreign ministers indeed urged Croatia to accelerate ICTY cooperation, yet they shied away from issuing an ultimatum nor threatened to impose sanctions; a similarly lenient approach was taken by the NATO secretary general Robertson one month later (cf. Altmann/Kasch 2002: 4; Hedl 2002; Southeast European Times 2002). Instead, some EU diplomats stressed that Croatia's membership would be conditional upon the transfer of indicted war criminals, while Greek's foreign minister, George Papandreu, reminded his colleagues that the threats had to be credible and backed by incentives to make Croatia comply with EU conditionality (cf. NYT 2002c, 2003b).[91] Finally, the Netherlands and the UK – the only two EU member states who acted in any serious manner – increased the pressure when they refused to ratify the SAA in December 2002 due to Croatia's lackluster ICTY cooperation (cf. Pavlaković 2008: 457).[92] On the other hand, Sweden and Austria obviously did not regard Croatia's failure to comply with the Bobetko impediment a great impediment to further association, as they indicated their support for Croatia's EU bid

[89] Frustration about the continually high levels of unemployment, the overall bad living standard, the slow pace of integration into the EU as well as the HDZ's successful strategy to cash in on the war crimes issue led to a tremendous shift in voter preferences in comparison to the elections of 2000. Between September and November 2002, 22% of those polled stated they would back the HDZ if elections were to be held immediately, whereas only 20% said they would vote for Račan's SDP (cf. Pavlaković 2008: 457). Other polls also found steadily increasing support for the HDZ: from 5% in 2000 to 16% in May 2001, 23% in June 2002 and more than 30% in February 2003, which turned the HDZ into the most popular political party in Croatia (all numbers cited in Peskin/Boduszyński 2003: 1133).

[90] Inconsistent and lenient behavior could already be observed before. For example, in May 2002, a top-ranking British diplomat called on Gotovina to surrender, only to announce in the same breath a $5 million donation for the realization of legal, economic and educational reforms to adopt EU standards (cf. Peskin/Boduszyński 2003: 1131).

[91] Papandreu and several EU offiicals referred to the diminishing financial incentives offered by the EU which would also undermine the Union's credibility, not to forget that the Balkans at that time rather came second as the attention of the EU and its member states at the time focused on Iraq (cf. NYT 2003b).

[92] Apart from that, the UK also refused to receive Croatia's foreign minister, Picula, during his "goodwill-tour" throughout European capitals, whereas he enjoyed a warm-hearted welcome by the French government that also spared him any unpleasant critique (cf. Altmann/Kasch 2002. 5).

submitted on 21 February 2003 (cf. Peskin/Boduszyński 2003: 1134).[93] Thinking rationally, the EU was aware of the danger of backfiring in case too much external pressure would lead to the downfall of the socio-liberal coalition since a likely nationalist successor government would have substantially limited the EU's leverage on Croatia as well as in the WB in general. The fact that the global awareness of Croatian atrocities has received relatively scant attention and thus has remained limited as well as traditionally close ties with Western states may have additionally contributed to the EU's overcautious approach. On the other hand, it appears doubtful whether the EU member states were actually able to credibly threaten Croatia with financial sanctions as they had a strong self-interest not to risk Croatia's economic and financial prosperity.[94] Therefore, the postponement of EU and NATO membership essentially was the only effective tool to ensure Croatia's ICTY cooperation and it was to be applied soon.

In the end, with Ademi's voluntary surrender the Račan government only served one of the three ICTY indictments against Croatian generals issued during its term of office.[95] Meanwhile, Gotovina was still on the run, while in November 2002 it was disclosed by an investigative *Globus* article that in the 16 months since the unsealing of the indictment, "not a single security agency had been issued instructions to locate and arrest Gotovina" (Pavlaković 2008: 459).[96] Yet it should turn out that not only Račan, but also the successive Sanader government would for a long time shy away from tightening measures for his arrest.

4.2.3 Phase II: The Sanader government (2003-2009)

On 22 December 2003, the HDZ won the parliamentary elections.[97] The next day, Sanader formed a minority government, supported by several smaller parties and including ethnic

93 Also German chancellor Gerhard Schröder, in October 2003, insisted that the failure to hand over Gotovina should not be an impediment to Croatia's EU accession. During a visit in Zagreb he declared that "Croatia is co-operating. [...] You cannot arrest someone who isn't there [...] and there should be more understanding of this" (cited in BBC 2003b). Schröder repeated this view in October 2004, when once again it came to heated debates on how strictly the conditionality principle should be applied (cf. The Guardian 2004b).

94 Croatia did not obtain major credits by the IMF and 94% of its bank deposits originated from Germany, Italy and Austria (cf. Altmann/Kasch 2002: 6). Moreover, the EU member states via the European Bank for Reconstruction and Development (EBRD) made higher investments in Croatia than in any other country in CEE (cf. ibid.).

95 Ivica Rajić, a Bosnian Croat who was arrested by Croatian authorities on 5 April 2003 had already been indicted by the ICTY in 1995 (cf. UNSC 2003: 51, 53). His arrest took place in Split, although the Račan government had previously argued that he was not in Croatia (cf. Pavlaković 2008: 459).

96 Moreover, in June 2003 Gotovina was able to give an interview to Nacional, while the Croatian authorities insisted they would not know about his whereabouts (cf. Pavlaković 2008: 449). Subsequently, Mesić tried in vain to convince the general to turn himself in voluntarily while he, like Račan, was afraid to resort to violence to arrest him for fear of political costs (cf. ibid.). Besides, even Mesić occasionally admitted that Gotovina probably had spent some time in Croatia while he was on the run (cf. ibid.: 474).

97 The HDZ obtained 66 out of the 152 parliamentary seats, whereas 88 deputies opted for the Sanader government (cf. BBC 2003c). See table 4 in the annex for the results of the 2003 parliamentary elections.

Serbian parliamentarians, while he pledged ICTY cooperation and made EU integration the linchpin of the government program (cf. Batt 2004; BBC 2003c).[98] In line with Sanader's intention, after its comeback to power the HDZ gradually moved away from extremism and transformed into a more moderate center-right party which also accelerated the marginalization of other extremist and anti-European parliamentary veto-players (cf. BTI 2003: 5, 2006: 5-6, 11-14, 2008: 9-10, 17-20; Jovic 2009: 16).[99] However, Mesić in the wake of his reelection in January 2005 warned that the HDZ's return to power had strengthened extremist forces, e.g. within the security apparatus, still operating behind the scenes (cf. Financial Times 2005a).[100] On 24 February 2004, two sealed indictments for Mladen Markač and Ivan Čermak arrived in Zagreb. Accompanied by the announcement to assist in their defense,[101] the Sanader government "acted immediately [...] and facilitated surrender of all accused" (UNSC 2004: 68).[102] This cooperative move was appreciated by the tribunal prosecutor who, in April 2004, declared that Croatia was now cooperating fully with the ICTY (cf. UNSC 2005: 36). In light of Del Ponte's positive assessment, the Commission subsequently issued a positive Opinion on Croatia's bid to join the EU (Commission 2004b); in June 2004 Croatia was granted candidate status (European Council 2004a: point *1.7* 31.). Moreover, the prosecutor's evaluation also satisfied the Netherlands and the UK who now signed the SAA which entered into effect on 1 February 2005 (cf. Commission 2005b: 105; Wichmann 2007: 86). Remarkably, no major public protests against the two extraditions were launched and also resistance from right-wing politicians remained limited (cf. Pavlaković

[98] The fact that the war crimes issue and ICTY cooperation was "virtually absent from the campaigns of the major political parties" (Pavlaković 2008: 460) can be attributed to strategic calculations. While the socio-liberal coalition parties were keen to mostly ignore those topics most beneficial to the mobilization of the rightist opposition, Sanader was aware that strengthening more radical forces would put at risk his goal to turn the HDZ into a more moderate conservative party, and, furthermore, potentially increase his future domestic political costs as he realistically anticipated that it would be inevitable to concede on ICTY cooperation in the course of EU rapprochement (ibid.). Thus, keeping in mind also the resistance in the Bobetko case, it appears doubtful whether from the absence of the war crimes issue from Sanader's campaign the inference can be drawn that veto players "since 2002 at the latest" were too weak to influence Sanader's preferences as indicated by Freyburg and Richter (2010: 273).

[99] Consequently, in the 2007 parliamentary elections the Croatian Party of Rights (HSP) won only one seat (out of 153). On the other hand, although Croatia's political elites in general took a pro-European stance, in the wake of elections they sharpened their political language to capitalize on the considerable amount of Euroscepticism, apparently thriving mostly due to widespread fears of losing national identity and sovereignty (cf. Devrim/Maršić 2009: 3; Madunić 2009: 28, 31). See tables 5 and 6 in the annex in the annex for an illustration of the marginalization of radical parties in national elections.

[100] Following an unequivocal pro-European campaign, Mesić had won the elections by a clear margin as an independent candidate (cf. Financial Times 2005a). See table 7 in the annex for the results of Croatia's presidential elections of 16 January 2005.

[101] Croatia's justice minister, Vesna Škare-Ožbolt, declared that "[t]he Croatian government is convinced of their innocence and will provide all the legal, technical and other means for their defence" (cited in BBC 2004b).

[102] Mladen Markač and Ivan Čermak turned themselves in on 11 March 2004 (cf. UNSC 2004: 67). Moreover, two weeks before the Commission was to issue its Opinion on Croatia's bid for membership, on 5 April 2004 six Bosnian Croats surrendered and subsequently left for The Hague, namely Jadranko Prlić, Bruno Stojić, Slobodan Praljak, Milivoj Petković, Valentin Ćorić and Berislav Pusić (cf. ibid.).

2008: 461). It appeared that Sanader's political adoption costs were relatively low in comparison to the previous social-liberal government as the HDZ could build on its conservative, nationalist credibility which was further strengthened by its official strategy for ICTY cooperation.[103] Besides, Sanader's symbolic nationalist moves played well domestically.[104] Moreover, Sanader could build on an informal political agreement with the main opposition parties, led by Račan's SDP, to cooperate on those issues that would be crucial to realize Croatia's accession to the EU (cf. Jovic 2009: 22; Pavlaković 2008: 461). The political costs regarding compliance with EU conditionality on the Markač and Čermak indictments therefore were rather low.

In December 2004, the EU scheduled the start of formal membership talks with Croatia on 17 March 2005, reiterating that "the remaining indictee [Gotovina] must be located and transferred to The Hague as soon as possible" (European Council 2004b: point *I.6* 15., cf. 2004a: point *I.7* 33.). The Sanader government, however, continued to send rather ambiguous messages to Brussels about its determination to actively seek his arrest.[105] While the Croatian officials claimed that he had left the country, Del Ponte insisted that "according to information coming from a lot of directions" Gotovina was still in Croatia (cited in BBC 2005a), adding that networks to protect war crimes suspects "were deeply embedded in Croatia's government structures" (cited in Financial Times 2005b).[106] In February 2005 Sanader and Mesić "for the first time publicly vowed to work together on the Gotovina issue", whereas only in March 2005 Gotovina was put on the wanted list and measures were taken to freeze his assets – immediately prior to when membership talks were scheduled to begin

[103] In July 2004, Sanader declared his government would pursue four goals regarding ICTY cooperation: to defend the "truth" about the 'Homeland War' and to rectify incorrect and unjustified charges, to assist in the defense of those who stand trial, to enable indicted Croats to defend themselves, and to accomplish the shift of all lawsuits involving indicted Croats from The Hague to domestic courts (cf. Pavlaković 2008: 461). T achieve these aims, the Sanader government repeatedly tried in vain to act as amicus curiae, amongst others in the Gotovina et al. case (cf. Amnesty International 2007: 24-25; Commission 2007a: 15; Jungvirth 2006).

[104] For example, he personally welcomed Blaškić back home in Zagreb following his release on 29 June 2004 after the tribunal's appeal chamber had overruled his judgment (cf. Del Ponte 2008: 337).Notwithstanding the numerous atrocities committed by Croat paramilitary troops in Bosnia, the Croatian government reportedly spent up to $20 million on Blaškić's defense before the appeals chamber (cf. Jungvirth 2006).

[105] For example, Miomir Žužul, Croatia's foreign minister, in a telling BBC interview in February 2004 refused to unequivocally answer questions about the Gotovina case, but labeled it "difficult [...] because of its political nature" (BBC 2004a). The Croatian foreign ministry, on the other hand, in a letter to the EU presidency in February 2005 pledged to do its "utmost" to cooperate on the "unavoidable obligation" to track down Gotovina (cited in BBC 2005a). Mesić, however, insisted it was impossible to comply with EU conditionality as the general was not on Croatian territory, adding that "[t]here is no one in the Croatia government who is helping Mr Gotovina" (cited in Financial Times 2005b). There were officials, he admitted, "but there are no longer" (ibid.).

[106] The prosecutor's allegations were supported, amongst others, by the British and American intelligence, whereas Croatia's credibility was derogated by a series of indiscreet actions through which sensitive information was leaked, apparently by renegade elements within Croatian intelligence (cf. BBC 2005b, 2005c; The Guardian 2004a, 2005b, 2005c).

(Pavlaković 2008: 463; cf. The Guardian 2005a).[107] Following Del Ponte's negative assessment of cooperation in March 2005,[108] the Council on 16 March 2005 decided to postpone accession talks, while it pointed out that they could open as soon as it was proved that Croatia was cooperating fully with the ICTY (cf. Council of the European Union 2005: 7-8).[109] Thus, despite 'parallel conditionality' by the US (cf. BBC 2003a; The Guardian 2005a),[110] the Sander government opted for noncompliance that spurred wide international condemnation and jeopardized its ability to keep its promise of EU integration (cf. The Guardian 2005a).

On the one hand, the government anticipated political costs,[111] given the unpopularity of ICTY cooperation and due to the fact that Gotovina during his years in hiding could build on a network of influential veto-players, made up of members of the Catholic church,[112] local and national deputies, organized crime rings, most of the Croatian media[113] and former comrades of the foreign legion now active in the French secret service (cf. Del Ponte 2008: 333, 346-349; NYT 2003c; The Guardian 2005a). On the other hand, owing to the HDZ's nationalist legacy, the government was not directly threatened in its political survival and thus costs remained rather moderate. Yet evidently the Croatian authorities did not regard the EU's

[107] Already in late 2003 the tribunal learned from President Mesić that the Croatian government had not suspended its financial support for Gotovina, nor frozen his financial assets and that Gotovina's wife kept receiving her husband's military pension (cf. Del Ponte 2008: 333).

[108] The ICTY declared that since the EU's positive opinion on Croatia's membership bid in April 2004, the Sanader government "did not do everything possible" to yield substantial results in the Gotovina case, "hoping that the fugitive would surrender voluntarily" (cf. UNSC 2005: 36).

[109] The Council decision, however, was taken amid bitter divisions between EU governments. While 12 member states, including Germany, France, Italy, the Netherlands and Great Britain alluded to the conditionality principle, a minority of states, including the four neighbor states Slovenia, Austria, Slovakia and Hungary argued for the opening of membership talks (cf. BBC 2005d, The Guardian 2005b; Wichmann 2007: 86).

[110] However, allegedly the Sanader government doubted the credibility of Washington's threats as apparently Gotovina reportedly was "working closely with American advisers" on operation "Storm" (NYT 2008; cf. Altmann/Kasch 2002: 6; Bartlett 2003: 69-70; Vujčić 2006: 3). Moreover, NATO troops and American intelligence repeatedly shied away of arresting war crimes indictees in the region in fear of high casualties as Carl Bildt, former envoy of the UN in Bosnia, had revealed (cf. BBC 2008a, 2008b; Peskin/Boduszyński 2003: 1120). Finally, the US has been opposed to the idea that an International Criminal Court (ICC) as an allegedly politicized body might indict American soldiers; thus it not only had an interest in winning Croatia as an opponent against the ICC but also used a similar argumentation as Croatia regarding the potential weaknesses of international tribunals, thereby downgrading the resonance of ICTY conditionality (cf. Altmann/Kasch 2002: 6; Peskin/ Boduszyński 2003: 1134).

[111] For about 80% of the population Gotovina continued to be a war hero in spring 2005 (cf. The Guardian 2005a). Moreover, in May 2005 Branimir Glavaš, who so for had been crucial for securing the support of the harder right-wing of the HDZ, withdrew support from Sanader and thus complicated government work (cf. Schimmelfennig 2008: 929).

[112] For example, Zlatko Sudac, a Catholic priest, in a right-wing newspaper advised Gotovina not to surrender while he admitted that the accused sought shelter on his island after the indictment had been issued (cf. Pavlaković 2008: 463-464). For an illustration of the obstructing role of the Catholic church regarding war crimes issues also see Bremer (2008), Del Ponte 2008 (346-349) and ICG (2001b: 8-9).

[113] The continued unwillingness among Croatians to face the dark sides of the 'Homeland War' at least to some extent may be attributed to the fact that "Croatian media completely marginalized The Hague-related issues" and that war crimes committed by Croatians "were covered very little and very superficially" in Croatia's major daily and on state-owned television (Obradovic 2002; see also Klarin 2009)

threats credible and thus expected to be treated with leniency – apparently in light of the often inconsistent way powerful member states had applied ICTY conditionality toward Croatia before.[114] Obviously they overlooked that this time not only the EU's credibility toward Croatia was at stake, but that the EU's strategy had much deeper ramifications as it was directly linked to the aim to track down Mladić and Karadžić.[115] To provide for Serbia's compliance regarding the two most wanted fugitives and to prove that the ICTY did not pursue a one-sided policy against Serbia, both the EU and Del Ponte urgently needed to put a high-ranking Croatian indictee on trial in The Hague (cf. Pavlaković 2008: 458, 468).[116]

The decision to convene accession talks was reached during the EU summit on 2/3 October 2005, despite the fact that Gotovina remained a fugitive (Council of the European Union 2008). Just hours before, following her visit to Zagreb on 30 September 2005, Del Ponte had informed EU officials that the Sanader government was now cooperating fully with the tribunal (cf. Blockmans 2007: 286; Del Ponte 2008: 349-351).[117] On 7 December 2005 Gotovina was finally arrested, according to Del Ponte due to a decisive hint by the Sanader government dating back to September 2005 (cf. Del Ponte 2008: 349-351; The Guardian 2005e, 2005f; UNSC 2006: 20). With the postponement of membership talks the EU had consistently applied the conditionality principle and thus credibility now was high. Moreover, high benefits in close reach trumped moderate adoption costs. Owing to the HDZ's nationalist credibility, domestic veto-players did not threaten to overturn the government while the fact that his arrest took place in Tenerife, i.e. outside of Croatia, further limited the costs of Croatian authorities as they did not have to extradite him.

[114] Seemingly, Sanader and Mesić simply could not imagine that the EU would risk to trigger a diplomatic crisis that, as Mesić framed it, would "breed euroscepticism" and impair the credibility of EU incentives by penalizing Croatia that, in relation to Bosnia and Serbia, provided "an example showing the region that it pays to adopt EU standards" (cited in The Guardian 2005b).

[115] Moreover, the EU understood that compliance with its Regional Approach played a vital role for yielding satisfactory results with regard to individual indictments, as e.g., the Serbian government's (non)cooperation on access to documents would have "clear implications for the ICTY trials concerning crimes in Croatia and Bosnia" (cf. Commission 2004a: 19-20; see also ibid. 2007b: 17-18, 2008: 15; 2009a: 16; UNSC 2002: 39-40).

[116] In a letter to the Financial Times, Denis MacShane, the former British minister for the Western Balkans (2001-2005), explicitly stated that any compromise toward Croatia in the Gotovina issue would make it "impossible to insist that the Serbs cooperate fully" with the ICTY (Financial Times 2005d). Besides, in reference to a possible linkage of Croatia's and Turkey's bids to join the EU, he unmistakably warned of any new forms of "horse-trading on questions of principle" that had led to the dreadful Balkan politics of the 1990s (cf. ibid.).

[117] Immediately prior to the EU summit, however, an emergency summit had to be called since Austria, while criticizing the EU's "double standards with Croatia" (cited in Financial Times 2005c), threatened to veto the opening of accession talks with Turkey scheduled for 3 October 2005. Apparently, Austria's concession on Turkey could only be assured on the condition that accession negotiations with Croatia started at the same time (cf. BBC 2005e, 2005f; The Guardian 2005d). Tribunal officials subsequently denied any suggestions that Del Ponte's sudden shift of opinion on Croatia's ICTY cooperation had been the result of heavy political pressure, giving tactical reasons instead to make sure that the foreseeable capture of Gotovina would not be frustrated (cf. Hartmann 2009: 71).

5. Conclusion

In line with earlier findings of Schimmelfennig (2008), rationalist argumentation with its focus on external incentives and domestic adoption costs is able to explain a great deal of the variation in Croatia's compliance with ICTY-related EU conditionality. Moreover, the case study has clearly illustrated the close interdependence between enlargement negotiations on the European level and domestic politics, i.e. the internal-external linkage of democratization. Yet in contrast to the assumptions made in recent studies (Freyburg/Richter 2010: 265; Schimmelfennig 2008: 929) my findings suggest that EU conditionality was rather inconsistently applied toward Croatia. Two main conclusions can be made from this. First, individual member states have gained in influence over enlargement policy that leads to a more politicized use of the conditionality tool and thus potentially hampers the EU's ability to provide for the necessary credibility and may lead to a conflict of goals and strategies (cf. Jovic 2009, Richter 2009a). Second, it illustrates the need to examine conjunctures and to place politics in time to "identify flaws in possible explanations" (Pierson 2004: 167; see also Rajkovic 2007). To provide more substantial explanations, it may also be necessary to go beyond purely rationalist argumentation, i.e. the "unconscious metaphysics it tacitly presupposes" (Whitehead 1933: 197). In this regard, to examine the role of 'national identity' out of a constructivist angle as done by Freyburg and Richter (2010) is theoretically sound as ICTY cooperation was inherently linked to Croatia's war of independence and thus touched on the very core of national sovereignty and self-definition. Moreover, empirically, the fact that Croatia has only insufficiently complied with EU rules on war crimes issues once Gotovina as the last remaining indictee had left for The Hague, highlights the pivotal role of constructivist concepts of identity formation, while also pointing out the need for credible conditionality to put forward reforms and influence domestic debates (cf. Subotić 2009).[118] Nonetheless, the empirical testing of their hypotheses has not been entirely convincing as Freyburg and Richter (2010) did not test against alternative (rationalist) explanations that would consider Sanader's references to national identity as 'rhetorical action' (Schimmelfennig 2003: 194-228) or as a means to strategically use domestic and international constraints to broaden his respective 'win-sets' in the 'two-level game' of accession negotiations (Grodsky 2009; Putnam 1988). Apart from that, more in-depth research is needed to certify if and why "partial identity change" actually took place (cf. CNN 2005; Vujčić

[118] In July 2009, when Sanader resigned, Croatian authorities had still not handed over important documents crucial for the preparation of the Gotovina et al. trial (cf. Richter 2009: 16; UNSC 2007: 18, 2008: 17, 2009: 17). Besides, the Sanader government fell short of implementing satisfying war crimes trials domesticall (Amnesty International 2009: 8-12; Commission 2009a: 35-37, 2009b: 7-11).

2006), and why in one case (Gotovina) the "identity conflict" ultimately was resolved in favor of compliance while obstructing it in the case of a much less prominent figure (Glavaš) (cf. Freyburg and Richter 2010: 275). Thus, many questions remain unanswered. Yet a better understanding on socialization mechanisms would be necessary to provide for implementation and internalization of norms as the only means to provide for effective EU integration and more thorough democratization both in Croatia and the region.

6. Annex

Table 1: The external incentives model (EIM) and alternative mechanisms of rule transfer

Principal actor in rule adoption process	Logic of rule adoption	
	Logic of consequences	Logic of appropriateness
EU-driven	External incentives model	Social learning model
Domestically-driven	Lesson-drawing model	Lesson-drawing model

Note: "Domestically driven" is denoted "CEEC-driven" in the original.
Source: Schimmelfennig and Sedelmeier (2005b: 8)

Table 2: Current position of the Western Balkan countries in the EU enlargement process***

	SAA negotiations opened	SAA signed	SAA in force	Interim Agreement in force	Official candidate	Applied for membership	Start of accession negotiations
Albania	2003 (Jan.)	2006 (June)	2009 (1 April)	Yes (Dec. 2006)	No	Yes (28 April 2009)	No
BiH	2005 (Nov.)	Initialed in 2007 (Dec.), signed in 2008 (June)	No	Signed in June 2008, in force since 1 July 2008	No	No	No
Croatia	2000 (Nov.)	2001 (Oct.)	2005 (Feb.)	Yes (1 March 2001)	Yes (June 2004)	Yes (21 Feb. 2003)	Yes (Oct. 2005)
FYR Macedonia	2000 (March)	2001 (April)	2004 (April)	Yes (June 2001)	Yes (Dec. 2005)	Yes (22 March 2004)	No date given
Montenegro	2006 (Sept.)	2007 (Oct.)	2010 (1 May)	Yes (Jan. 2008)	No	Yes (15 Dec. 2008)	No
Serbia	2005 (Oct.)	Initialed in 2007 (Nov.), signed in 2008 (Apr.)	No	Signed (Apr. 2008), but not in force yet	No	Yes (22 Dec. 2009)	No

*** Last update on 3 September 2010
Source: Homepage of the European Commission: http://ec.europa.eu/enlargement/index_en.htm (accessed on 11 August 2013)

Table 3: Results of the parliamentary elections in Croatia (3 January 2000)

Party	Seats
Social Democratic Party - Croatian Social Liberal Party (SDP-HSLS)	71
Croatian Democratic Union (HDZ)	46
Opposition Four (HSS, LS, HSS, IDS)	24
Croatian Party of Rights / Croatian Christian Democratic Union (HSP/HKDU)	5

Notes: The coalition government was built by the SDP-HSLS coalition and the so-called Opposition Four (HSS, LS; HSS; IDS). In total there were 151 parliamentary seats at stake, while the data of Election Guide represents only the results of the main parties and thus neglects five seats.

Source: Election Guide http://www.electionguide.org/results.php?ID=612 (accessed on 3 September 2010)

Table 4: Results of the parliamentary elections in Croatia (22 December 2003)

Party	valid votes	% [of valid votes]	seats
Croatian Democratic Union (HDZ)	840,692	33.91 %	66
Social Democratic Party of Croatia (SDP), Istrian Democratic Assembly (IDS), Liberal Party, LIBRA	560,593	22.61 %	43
Croatian People's Party (HNS), Croatian Party of Slavonia and Baranja (SBHS) and the Alliance of Primorje and Gorski Kotar (PGS)	198,781	8.02 %	11
Croatian Peasant Party (HSS)	177,359	7.15 %	9
Croatian Party of Rights (HSP) and the Zagorje Democratic Party (ZDS)	157,987	6.37 %	8
Croatian Social Liberal Party (HSLS) and Democratic Center (DC)	100,335	4.05 %	3
Croatian Pensioners Party (HSU)	98,537	3.97 %	3
Croatian Democratic Peasant Party (HDSS)	24,872	1.00 %	1
Others	319,811	12.90 %	0

Source: Election Guide. http://www.electionguide.org/results.php?ID=396 (accessed on 11 August 2013)

Table 5: Left-Right composition of the Croatian parliament 1990-2003

Position	1990	1992	1995	2000	2003
Left	25.0	-	-	-	-
Left center	-	13.2	12.6	34.3	34.9
Centre	3.8	10.1	9.4	15.9	4.0
Right center	-	2.2	7.9	10.6	50.0
Right	68.8	65.2	62.2	33.8	5.3

Notes: Left = unreformed post-communists (Social Democratic Party of Croatia (SDP) 1990)); Left center = social democrats/reformed communists, left liberals (SDP since 1992, Croatian People's Party (HNS), Istrian Democratic Assembly (IDS), Liberal Party (LS)); Center = liberals, centrist democrats (Coalition of People's Agreement (KNS), Croatian Social Liberal Party (HSLS), Democratic Center (DC), Croatian Party of Pensioners (HSU)); Right center = conservatives, moderate nationalists (Croatian Peasants' Party (HSS), Croatian Democratic Union (HDZ) since 2003)); Right = extremist nationalists, right radicals (HDZ 1990-2000, Croatian Party of Rights (HSP)); difference to 100 per cent = minor parties, minority and independent MPs.

Source: Zakošek (2008: 601)

Table 6: Results of the parliamentary elections in Croatia (25 November 2007)

Party	Valid Votes	% [of Valid Votes]	Seats (153 in total)
Croatian Democratic Union (HDZ)	834,203	34.91 %	66
Social Democratic Party of Croatia (SDP), Istrian Democratic Assembly (IDS), Liberal Party, LIBRA	776,656	32.50 %	56
Croatian People's Party (HNS)	168,439	7.05 %	7
Croatian Social Liberal Party / Croatian Peasant Party (HSLS/HSS) ***	161,813	6.77 %	8
Croatian Pensioner Party/Democratic Party of Pensioners (HSU/DSU)	101,091	4.23 %	1
Croatian Party of Rights (HSP)	83,006	3.47 %	1
Croatian Democratic Congress of Slavonia and Baranja (HDSSB)	44,552	1.86 %	3
Istrian Democratic Assembly (IDS)	38,267	0.00 %	3
Independent Democratic Serb Party (SDSS)	9,115	0.38 %	3
Other Parties	151,412	6.34 %	0
Independents	20,837	0.87 %	5

*** The Croatian Social Liberal Party received 2 seats. The Croatian Peasant Party received 6 seats.

Source: Election Guide. http://www.electionguide.org/results.php?ID=1146 (accessed on 11 August 2013)

Table 7: Results of the presidential elections in Croatia (16 January 2005, second and final round)

Candidates	Party	Valid Votes	% [of Valid Votes]
Stjepan Mesić	Social Democratic Party of Croatia (SDP)	1,454,451	65.93%
Jadranko Kosor	Croatian Democratic Union (HDZ)	751,692	34.07%

Source: Election Guide. http://www.electionguide.org/results.php?ID=68 (accessed on 11 August 2013)

7. Bibliographical references

7.1 Literature

Altmann, Franz-Lothar / Kasch, Holger (2002): *Kroatien am Scheideweg? Der Fall Bobetko als Prüfstein der Außen- und Innenpolitik.* SWP Aktuell 47, November 2002, Stiftung Wissenschaft und Politik (SWP), Berlin. http://www.swp-berlin.org/produkte/swp_aktuell_detail.php?id=1940 (accessed on 3 September 2010).

Bartlett, William (2003): *Croatia: Between Europe and the Balkans.* London / New York.

Batt, Judy (2004): *Summary: Serbia and Croatia: after the elections.* Analysis No. 0, April 2004, European Union Institute for Security Studies (EUISS), Paris. http://www.iss.europa.eu/index.php?id=18&no_cache=1&tx_ttnews[pointer]=4&tx_ttnews[tt_news]=576&tx_ttnews[backPid]=132&cHash=526dc3e004 (accessed on 3 September 2010).

Bennett, Andrew / Elman, Colin (2006): *Qualitative Research: Recent Developments in Case Study Methods.* In: Annual Review of Political Science,. 9, 455-476.

Bennett, Andrew / Elman, Colin (2007): *Case Study Methods in the International Relations Subfield.* In: Comparative Political Studies, 40(2), 170-195.

Bertelsmann Transformation Index (BTI) (2003): *Croatia.* Bertelsmann Stiftung, Gütersloh. http://bti2006.bertelsmann-transformation-index.de/170.0.html?L=1 (accessed on 3 September 2010).

Bertelsmann Transformation Index (BTI) (2006): *Croatia.* Bertelsmann Stiftung, Gütersloh. http://bti2006.bertelsmann-transformation-index.de/170.0.html?L=1 (accessed on 3 September 2010).

Bertelsmann Transformation Index (BTI) (2008): *Croatia Country Report.* Bertelsmann Stiftung, Gütersloh. http://www.bertelsmann-transformation-index.de/170.0.html?&L=1 (accessed on 3 September 2010).

Beyme, Klaus von (2001): *Institutional Engineering and Transition to Democracy,* in: Jan Zielonka, Jan (ed.): *Democratic Consolidation in Eastern Europe Volume 1: Institutional Engineering.* Oxford: 3-24.

Bicanic, Ivo / Franicevic, Vojmir (2003): *Understanding Reform: the Case of Croatia.* Global Development Network Southeast Europe (GDN-SEE), November 2003. http://www.wiiw.ac.at/balkan/files/GDN_UnderstandingReform_Croatia.pdf (accessed on 3 September 2010).

Bikhchandani, Sushil / Hirshleifer, David / Welch, Ivo (1998): *Learning from the Behavior of Others: Conformity, Fads, and Informational Cascades.* In: The Journal of Economic Perspectives, 12(3), 151-170.

Birch, Sarah (2003): *Electoral Systems and Political Transformation in Post-Communist Europe*. Basingstoke: 28-51.

Blockmans, Steven (2007): *Tough Love: The European Union's Relations with the Western Balkans*. The Hague.

Börzel, Tanja (2006): *Coping with Accession – New Modes and EU Enlargement*. In: Gunnar Schuppert (ed.): *The Europeanisation of Governance*. Baden-Baden, 77-92.

Börzel, Tanja (ed.) (2009a): *Coping with Accession to the European Union: New Modes of Environmental Governance*. Basingstoke.

Börzel, Tanja (2009b): *New Modes of Governance and Accession: The Paradox of Double Weakness*. In: Tanja Börzel (ed.): *Coping with Accession to the European Union: New Modes of Environmental Governance*. Basingstoke, 7-31.

Börzel, Tanja (2010): *The Transformative Power of Europe Reloaded: The Limits of External Europeanization*. KFG Working Paper Series, No. 11, February 2010.
http://www.polsoz.fu-berlin.de/en/v/transformeurope/publications/working_paper/WP_11_February_Boerzel1.pdf
(accessed on 3 September 2010).

Börzel, Tanja / Risse, Thomas (2002): *Die Wirkung internationaler Institutionen: Von der Normanerkennung zur Normeinhaltung*. In: Markus Jachtenfuchs / Michèle Knodt (eds.): *Regieren in internationalen Institutionen*. Opladen, 141-181.

Börzel, Tanja / Risse, Thomas (2009): *The Transformative Power of Europe: The European Union and the Diffusion of Ideas*. KFG Working Paper Series, No. 1, May 2009, Berlin.
http://www.polsoz.fu-berlin.de/en/v/transformeurope/publications/working_paper/WP_01_Juni_Boerzel_Risse.pdf
(accessed on 3 September 2010).

Bremer, Thomas (2008): *The Catholic Church and its Role in Politics and Society*. In: Sabrina Ramet / Konrad Clewing / Reneo Lukić (eds.): *Croatia since Independence: War, Politics, Society, Foreign Relations*. Munich, 251-268.

Brkljačić, Maja (2003): *What Past is Present?* In: International Journal of Politics, Culture and Society, 17(1), 41-52.

Bunce, Valerie (2003): *Rethinking Recent Democratization: Lessons from the Postcommunist Experience*. In: World Politics, 55(2): 167-192.

Calic, Marie-Janine (2001): *Der Stabilitätspakt für Südosteuropa:Eine erste Bilanz*. In: Aus Politik- und Zeitgeschichte (APuZ), B 13-14/2001, 9-16.
http://www.bpb.de/files/JQWWME.pdf
(accessed on 3 September 2010).

Checkel, Jeffrey (1999): *Social Construction and Integration*. In: Journal of European Public Policy, 6(4), 545-560.

Checkel, Jeffrey (2001): *Why Comply? Social Learning and European Identity Change*. In: International Organization, 55(3), 553-588.

Checkel, Jeffrey (2005a): *International Institutions and Socialization in Europe: Introduction and Framework*. In: International Organization, 59(4), 801-826.

Checkel, Jeffrey (2005b): *It's the Process Stupid! Process Tracing in the Study of European and International Politics*. ARENA Working Paper, No. 26, October 2005. http://www.arena.uio.no/publications/working-papers2005/papers/wp05_26.pdf (accessed on 3 September 2010).

Cooley, Alexander (2003): *Western Conditions and Domestic Choices: The Influence of External Actors on the Post-Communist Transition*. In: Freedom House (ed.): *Nations in Transit 2003: Democratization in East Central Europe and Eurasia*. New York, 25-38. http://www.barnard.edu/polisci/faculty/cooley.html (accessed on 3 September 2010).

Cruvellier, Thierry / Valiñas, Marta (2006): *Croatia: Selected Developments in Transitional Justice*. International Center for Transitional Justice (ICTJ), New York, December 2006. http://www.ictj.org/static/Europe/TJdevelopments.eng.pdf (accessed on 3 September 2010).

Dallara, Cristina (2009): *Serbia: Borderline democracy?* In: Amichai Magen / Leonardo Morlino (eds.): *International Actors, Democratization and the Rule of Law: Anchoring Democracy?* New York, London, 156-188.

Del Ponte, Carla (2008): *Im Namen der Anklage: Meine Jagd auf Kriegsverbrecher und die Suche nach Gerechtigkeit*. Frankfurt am Main.

Devrim, Deniz / Maršić, Tomislav (2009): *Croatia, Macedonia and the EU: Setting the Bar too High?* Notes Internacionals CIDOB No. 08, December 2009, Centro de Estudios y de Documentación Internacionales de Barcelona (CIDOB). http://www.cidob.org/index.php/es/publicaciones/notes_internacionals_cidob/n1_08/croatia_macedonia_and_the_eu_setting_the_bar_too_high (accessed on 3 September 2010).

DiMaggio, Paul / Powell, Walter (1991): *The Iron Cage Revisited: Institutional Isomorphism and Collective Rationality in Organizational Fields*. In: Walter Powell / Paul Di Maggio (eds.): *The New Institutionalism in Organizational Analysis*. Chicago / London, 63-82.

Diez, Thomas / Stetter, Stephan / Albert, Mathias (2006): *The European Union and Border Conflicts: The Transformative Power of Integration*. In: International Organization, 60(3), 563-593.

Elbasani, Arolda (2009): *EU Administrative Conditionality and Domestic Downloading: The Limits of Europeanization in Challenging Contexts*. KFG Working Paper Series, No. 2, Berlin. http://www.polsoz.fu-berlin.de/en/v/transformeurope/publications/working_paper/WP_02_July_Elbasani.pdf (accessed on 3 September 2010).

Elgie, Robert / Zielonka, Jan (2001): *Constitutions and Constitution-Building. A Comparative Perspective*. In: Jan Zielonka (ed.): *Democratic Consolidation in Eastern Europe: Volume I. Institutional Engineering*. Oxford: 25-47.

Emerson, Michael / Youngs, Richard (eds.) (2009): *Democracy's Plight in the European Neighbourhood: Struggling transitions and proliferating dynasties*. Centre for European Policy Studies (CEPS), 30 October 2009, Brussels.
http://www.ceps.be/book/democracy%E2%80%99s-plight-european-neighbourhood-struggling-transitions-and-proliferating-dynasties
(accessed on 3 September 2010).

Epstein, Rachel (2008a): *In Pursuit of Liberalism: International Institutions in Postcommunist Europe*. Baltimore.

Epstein, Rachel (2008b): *The social context in conditionality: internationalizing finance in postcommunist Europe*. In: Journal of European Public Policy, 15(6), 880-898.

Falkner, Gerda / Treib, Oliver (2008): *Three Worlds of Compliance or Four? The EU 15 Compared to New Member States*. In: Journal of Common Market Studies, 46(2), 293-313.

Fearon, James / Wendt, Alexander (2005): *Rationalism Vs. Constructivism: A Sceptical View*. In: Walter Carlsnaes / Thomas Risse / Beth Simmons (eds.): *Handbook of International Relations*. London, 52-72.

Fierro, Elena (2003): *The EU's Approach to Human Rights Conditionality in Practice*. The Hague.

Finnemore, Martha / Sikkink, Kathryn (1998): *International Norm Dynamics and Political Change*. In: International Organization, 52(4), 887-917.

Flockhart, Trine (ed.) (2005a): *Socializing Democratic Norms: The Role of International Organizations for the Construction of Europe*. Basingstoke.

Flockhart, Trine (2005b): *Socialization and Democratization: a Tenuous but Intriguing Link*. In: Trine Flockhart (ed.): *Socializing Democratic Norms: The Role of International Organizations for the Construction of Europe*. Basingstoke, 1-20.

Flockhart, Trine (2005c): *Complex Socialization and the Transfer of Democratic Norms*. In: Trine Flockhart (ed.): *Socializing Democratic Norms: The Role of International Organizations for the Construction of Europe*. Basingstoke, 43-62.

Freyburg, Tina / Richter, Solveig (2010): *National identity matters: the limited impact of EU political conditionality in the Western Balkans*. In: Journal of European Public Policy, 17(2), 263-281.

Gawrich, Andrea / Melnykovska, Inna / Schweickert, Rainer (2009): *Neighbourhood Europeanization through ENP: The Case of Ukraine*. KFG Working Paper Series, No. 3, August 2009.
http://www.polsoz.fu-berlin.de/en/v/transformeurope/publications/working_paper/WP_-03_August_Melnykovska_Gawrich_Schweickert.pdf
(accessed on 3 September 2010).

George, Alexander / Bennett, Andrew (2005): *Case Studies and Theory Development in the Social Sciences*, Cambridge.

Gerring, John (2007): *Case Study Research: Principles and Practices*. New York.

Goffman, Erving (1974): *Frame Analysis: An Essay on the Organization of Experience*. New York.

Goldstein, Ivo (1999): *Croatia: A History*. London.

Goodman, Ryan / Jinks, Derek (2003): *Towards an Institutional Theory of Sovereignty*. In: Stanford Law Review, 55(5), 1749-1788.

Gourevitch (1978): *The Second Image Reversed: the International Sources of Domestic Politics. I*n: International Organization, 32(4), 881-912.

Grabbe, Heather (2001): *How does Europeanisation affect CEE Governance?* In: Journal of European Public Policy, 8(6), 1013-1031.

Grabbe, Heather (2006): *The EU's Transformative Power: Europeanization Through Conditionality in Central and Eastern Europe*. New York.

Grodsky, Brian (2009): *Exploring the Schelling Conjecture in Reverse: 'International Constraints' and Cooperation with the International Criminal Tribunal for the former Yugoslavia*. 20 August 2009.
http://papers.ssrn.com/sol3/papers.cfm?abstract_id=1458728
(accessed on 3 September 2010).

Grugel, Jean (2005): *The 'International' in Democratization: Norms and the Middle Ground*. In: Trine Flockhart (ed.): *Socializing Democratic Norms: The Role of International Organizations for the Construction of Europe*. Basingstoke, 23-42.

Haggard, Stephan / Robert Kaufman (1997): *The Political Economy of Democratic Transitions*. In: Comparative Politics 29(3): 263-283.

Hartmann, Florence (2009): *The ICTY and EU conditionality*. In: Judy Batt / Jelena Obradovic-Wochnik (eds.): W*ar crimes, conditionality and EU integration in the Western Balkans*. Chaillot Paper No. 116, June 2009, European Union Institute for Security Studies (EUISS), Paris, 67-82.
http://www.iss.europa.eu/uploads/media/cp116.pdf
(accessed on 3 September 2010).

Havemann, Heather (1994): *Follow the Leader: Mimetic Isomorphism and Entry Into New Markets*. In: Administrative Science Quarterly, 38(4), 593-627.

Hedl, Drago (2002): *Croatia Faces Sanctions Over Bobetko*. Institute for War & Peace Reporting (IWPR), BCR Issue 375, 22 October 2002, Institute for War & Peace Reporting (IWPR), London / Washington D.C.
http://iwpr.net/report-news/croatia-faces-sanctions-over-bobetko
(accessed on 3 September 2010).

Hériter, Adrienne (2002): *New Modes of Governance in Europe: Policy-Making without Legislating?* In: Adrienne Héritier (ed.): *Common Goods, Reinventing European and International Governance.* Lanham, 185-206.

Hille, Peter / Knill, Christoph (2006): *'It's the Bureaucracy, Stupid': The Implementation of the Acquis Communautaire in EU Candidate Countries, 1999–2003.* In: European Union Politics, 7(4), 531-552.

Hofer, Stephan (2008): *Die Europäische Union als Regelexporteur: Dei Europäisierung der Energiepolitik in Bulgarien, Serbien und der Ukraine.* Baden-Baden.

Holzinger, Katharina / Jürgens, Helge / Knill, Christoph (eds.) (2007): *Transfer, Diffusion und Konvergenz von Politiken.* In: PVS Politische Vierteljahresschrift, Sonderheft 38, Wiesbaden.

ICG (2001a): *After Milosevic: A Practical Agenda for Lasting Balkans Peace.* Europe Report No. 108, 1 April 2001, International Crisis Group (ICG), Brussels. http://www.crisisgroup.org/en/regions/europe/balkans/108-after-milosevic-a-practical-agenda-for-lasting-balkans-peace.aspx (accessed on 3 September 2010).

ICG (2001b): *Croatia: Facing Up to War Crimes.* ICG Balkans Briefing Paper, 16 December 2001, International Crisis Group (ICG), Zagreb / Brussels. http://www.crisisgroup.org/~/media/Files/europe/Croatia%203.ashx (accessed on 3 September 2010).

Jacoby, Wade (2004): *The Enlargement of the European Union and NATO: Ordering from the Menu in Central Europe.* Cambridge .

Jansen, Stef (2002): *The Violence of Memories: Local narratives of the past after ethnic cleansing in Croatia.* In: Rethinking History, 6(1), 77-93.

Johnson, Juliet (2006): *Two-track diffusion and central bank embeddedness: the politics of Euro adoption in Hungary and the Czech Republic.* In: Review of International Political Economy, 13(3), 361-386.

Jovic, Dejan (2009): *Croatia after Tudjman: the ICTY and issues of transitional justice.* In: Judy Batt / Jelena Obradovic-Wochnik (eds.): *War crimes, conditionality and EU integration in the Western Balkans.*, Chaillot Paper, No. 116, June 2009, European Union Institute for Security Studies (EUISS), Paris, 13-27. http://www.iss.europa.eu/uploads/media/cp116.pdf (accessed on 3 September 2010).

Jungvirth, Goran (2006): *Croatia: Funding the Generals.* ICTY Tribunal Update No. 453, 22 May 2006, Institute for War & Peace Reporting (IWPR), London / Washington D.C. http://iwpr.net/report-news/croatia-funding-generals (accessed on 3 September 2010).

Jupille, Joseph / Caporaso, James / Checkel, Jeffrey (2003): *Integrating Institutions: Rationalism, Constructivism, and the Study of the European Union.* In: Comparative Political Studies, 36(1-2), 7-40.

Jünemann, Annette / Knodt, Michèle (eds.) (2007): *Externe Demokratieförderung durch die Europäische Union: European: European External Democracy Promotion*. Baden-Baden.

Kelley, Judith (2004a): *Ethnic Politics in Europe: The Power of Norms and Incentives*. Princeton.

Kelly, Judith (2004b): *International Actors on the Domestic Scene: Membership Conditionality and Socialization by International Institutions*. In: International Organization, 58(3), 425-457.

King, Gary / Keohane, Robert / Verba, Sidney (1994*): Designing Social Inquiry: Scientific Inference in Qualitative Research*. Princeton.

Klarin, Mirko (2009): *The Impact of the ICTY Trials on Public Opinion in the Former Yugoslavia*. In: Journal of International Criminal Justice, 7, 89-96.
http://jicj.oxfordjournals.org/cgi/reprint/7/1/89
(accessed on 27 August 2010).

Kuzovac, Zoran (2000): *The Prospects for Change in Post-Tudjman Croatia*. In: East European Constitutional Review, 9(3), 57-62.

Lakatos, Imre (1978): *The methodology of scientific research programmes: Philosophical Papers Volume 1*. Cambridge / London / New York.

Lavenex, Sandra (2004): *EU external governance in 'wider Europe'*. In: Journal of European Public Policy, 11(4), 680-700.

Lavenex, Sandra / Schimmelfennig, Frank (2009): *EU rules beyond EU borders: theorizing external governance in European politics*. In: Journal of European Public Policy, 16(6), 791-812.

Lavenex, Sandra / Uçarer, Emek (2004): *The External Dimension of Europeanization: The Case of Immigration Policies*. In: Cooperation and Conflict, 39(4): 417–443.

Leeds, Brett (1999): *Domestic Political Institutions, Credible Commitments, and International Cooperation*. In: American Political Science Review, 43(4), 979-1002.

Levitsky, Steven / Lucan, Way (2006): *Linkage versus Leverage: Rethinking the International Dimension of Regime Change*. In: Comparative Politics, 38(4), 379-400.

Linden, Ronald (ed.) (2002): *Norms and Nannies: The Impact of International Organizations on the Central and Eastern European States*. Lanham, Maryland.

Linz, Juan / Stepan, Alfred (1996): *„Stateness", Nationalism, and Democratization*. In: Juan Linz / Alfred Stepan (eds.): *Problems of Democratic Transitions and Consolidation*. Baltimore: 16-37.

Madunić, Josip (2009): *Euroskeptizismus in Kroatien: Gesellschaft und Politik im Widerspruch?* In: Südosteuropa Mitteilungen, 49(5), 18-33.

Magen, Amichai / Morlino, Leonardo (2009): *Hybrid regimes, the rule of law, and external influence on domestic change.* In: Amichai Magen / Leonardo Morlino (eds.): *International Actors, Democratization and the Rule of Law: Anchoring Democracy?* New York / London, 1-25.

Magen, Amichai / Risse, Thomas / McFaul, Michael (eds.) (2009): *Promoting Democracy and the Rule of Law: American and European Strategies*. Basingstoke.

March, James / Olsen, Johan (1998): *The Institutional Dynamics of International Political Orders*. In: International Organization, 52(4), 943-969.

Massari, Maurizio (2005): *Do All Roads Lead to Brussels? Analysis of the Different Trajectories of Croatia, Serbia-Montenegro and Bosnia-Herzegovina*. In: Cambridge Review of International Affairs, 18(2), 259-273.

Meyer, John / Rowan, Brian (1977): *Institutionalized Organizations: Formal Structures as Myth and Ceremony*. In: American Journal of Sociology 83(2), 340-363.

Moravcsik, Andrew (1993): *Introduction: Integrating International and Domestic Theories of International Bargaining*. In: Peter Evans / Robert Putnam (eds.): *Double-edged Diplomacy: International Bargaining and Domestic Politics*. Berkeley, 3-42.

Moravcsik, Andrew / Vachudova, Milada (2003): *National Interests, State Power and EU Enlargement*. In: East European Politics and Societies, 17(1), 42-57.

Morlino, Leonardo / Magen, Amichai (2009a): *A framework for analysis*. In: Amichai Magen / Leonardo Morlino (eds.): *International Actors, Democratization and the Rule of Law: Anchoring Democracy?* New York / London, 26-52.

Morlino, Leonardo / Magen, Amichai (2009b): *Scope, depth and limits of external influence: Conclusions*. In: Amichai Magen / Leonardo Morlino (eds.): *International Actors, Democratization and the Rule of Law: Anchoring Democracy?* New York / London, 224-258.

Mundis, Daryl (2001): *Reporting Non-Compliance: Rule 7bis*. In: Richard May et al. (eds.): *Essays on ICTY Procedure and Evidence in Honour of Gabrielle Kirk-MacDonald.* The Hague, 421-438.

Noutcheva, Gergana / Bechev, Dimitar (2008): *The Successful Laggards: Bulgaria's and Romania's Accession to the EU*. In: East European Politics and Societies, 22(1), 114-144.

Nwobike, Justice (2005): *The Application of Human Rights in African Caribbean and Pacific–European Union Development and Trade Partnership*. In: German Law Journal, 6(10), 1381-1406.
http://www.germanlawjournal.com/pdfs/Vol06No10/PDF_Vol_06_No_10_1381_1406_Developments_Nwobikefinal.pdf
(accessed on 27 July 2010).

Obradovic, Stojan (2002): I*CTY Coverage on Croatian Television and in Vecernji List: Covering up The Hague?* In: Media Online, Southeast European Media Journal, 14 January 2002. http://www.mediaonline.ba/en/?ID=175 (accessed on 27 August 2010).

Pavlaković, Vjeran (2008): *Better the Grave than a Slave: Croatia and the International Criminal Tribunal for the Former Yugoslavia.* In: Sabrina Ramet / Konrad Clewing / Reneo Lukić (eds.): *Croatia since Independence: War, Politics, Society, Foreign Relations.* Munich, 447-477.

Peskin, Victor / Boduszyński (2003): *International Justice and Domestic Politics: Post-Tudjman Croatia and the International Criminal Tribunal for the Former Yugoslavia.* In: Europe-Asia Studies, 55(7), 1117-1142.

Pevehouse, Jon (2005): *Democracy from Above: Regional Organizations and Democratization.* Cambridge.

Pierson, Paul (2004): *Politics in Time: history, institutions, and social analysis.* Princeton.

Pippan, Christian (2004): *The Rocky Road to Europe: The EU's Stabilisation and Association Process for the Western Balkans and the Principle of Conditionality.* In: European Foreign Affairs Review, 9(2), 219-245.

Polillo, Simone / Guillén, Mauro (2005): *Globalization Pressures and the State: The Worldwide Spread of Central Bank Independence.* In: American Journal of Sociology, 110(6), 1764-1802.

Pridham, Geoffrey (2007): *Change and Continuity in the European Union's Political Conditionality: Aims, Approach, and Priorities.* In: Democratization, 14(3), 446-471.

Pridham, Geoffrey (2008): *The EU's Political Conditionality and Post-Accession Tendencies: Comparisons from Slovakia and Latvia.* In: Journal of Common Market Studies, 46(2), 365-387.

Przeworski, Adam (1991): *Democracy and the Market: Political and Economic Reforms in Eastern Europe and Latin America.* Cambridge.

Putnam, Robert (1988): *Diplomacy and Domestic Politics: The Logic of Two Level Games.* In: International Organization 42(3), 427-60.

Radonic, Ljiljana (2007): *Die Konsolidierung einer defekten Demokratie? – Kroatien von 1990 bis heute.* Arbeitspapiere und Materialien Nr. 85, Forschungsstelle Osteuropa, Bremen, 23-26.
http://www.forschungsstelle.uni-bremen.de/index.php?option=com_content&task=blogcategory&id=45&Itemid=68 (accessed on 27 August 2010).

Rajkovic, Nikolas (2007): *The Limits of Consequentialism: ICTY Conditionality and (Non)Compliance in Post-Milosevic-Serbia.* Paper presented at the 6th Pan-European International Relations Conference, University of Turin, 12-15 September 2007. http://archive.sgir.eu/uploads/Rajkovic-the_limits_of_consequentialism-ecprtorino.pdf (accessed on 27 August 2010).

Ramet, Sabrina (2005): *Thinking about Yugoslavia: Scholarly Debates about the Yugoslav Breakup and the Wars in Bosnia and Kosovo.* Cambridge.

Ramet, Sabrina (2008): *Politics in Croatia since 1990*. In: Sabrina Ramet (ed.): *Serbia, Croatia and Slovenia at Peace and at War: Selected Writings, 1983-2007*. Berlin, 193-220.

Renner, Stephan (2009): *The Energy Community of Southeast Europe: A neo-functionalist project of regional integration*. In: European Integration Online Papers (EIoP), 13(1), 25 February 2009.
http://eiop.or.at/eiop/index.php/eiop/article/view/2009_001a
(accessed on 27 August 2010).

Renner, Judith / Horelt, Michel-André (2008): *"Of Heroes and Villains": Competing Identity-Constructions in Post-War Croatia*. Munich Working Papers in IR, No. 1, January 2008.
http://www.gsi.uni-muenchen.de/lehreinheiten/ls_ib/arbeitspapiere/wps/renner_horelt_2008.pdf
(accessed on 2 September 2010).

Richter, Solveig (2009a): *Zielkonflikte der EU-Erweiterungspolitik? Kroatien und Makedonien zwischen Stabilität und Demokratie*. SWP Studie S 19, July 2009, Stiftung Wissenschaft und Politik (SWP), Berlin.
http://www.swp-berlin.org/common/get_document.php?asset_id=6170
(accessed on 27 August 2010).

Richter, Solveig (2009b): *Zur Effektivität externer Demokratisierung: Die OSZE in Südosteuropa als Partner, Mahner, Besserwisser?* Baden-Baden.

Risse, Thomas (1999): *International Norms and Domestic Change: Arguing and Communicative Behavior in the Human Rights Area*. In: Politics and Society, 27(4), 529-559.

Risse, Thomas (2003): *Konstruktivismus, Rationalismus und Theorien Internationaler Beziehungen – warum empirisch nichts so heiß gegessen wird, wie es theoretisch gekocht wurde*. In: Gunter Hellmann / Klaus Dieter Wolf / Michael Zürn (eds.): *Die neuen Internationalen Beziehungen: Forschungsstand und Perspektiven in Deutschland*. Baden-Baden, 99-132.

Rontoyanni, Clelila / Korosteleva, Elena (2005): *Belarus: an Authoritarian Exception from the Model of Post-Communist Democratic Transition?* In: Trine Flockhart (ed.): *Socializing Democratic Norms: The Role of International Organizations for the Construction of Europe*. Basingstoke, 209-231.

Ruggie, John (1998): *What makes the world hang together? Neo-utilitarianism and the social constructivist challenge*. In: International Organization, 52(4), 855-885.
http://faculty.msb.edu/murphydd/CRIC/Readings/Ruggie--Social%20Constructivist%20Challenge%20(Hanging%20Together)%201998.pdf
(accessed on 27 August 2010).

Sasse, Gwendolyn (2005): *EU Conditionality and Minority Rights: Translating the Copenhagen Criterion into Policy*. EUI Working Papers, RSCAS No. 2005/16, European University Institute (EUI), Florence.
http://www.eui.eu/RSCAS/WP-Texts/05_16.pdf
(accessed on 27 August 2010). Scharpf, Fritz (1997): *Games Real Actors Play: Actor-Centred Institutionalism in Policy-Research*. Boulder.

Schelling, Thomas (1998): *Social mechanisms and social dynamics*. In: Peter Hedström / Richard Swedberg (eds.): *Social Mechanisms: An Analytical Approach to Social Theory*. Cambridge, 32-44.

Schimmelfennig, Frank (2003): *The EU, NATO and the Integration of Europe: Rules and Rhetoric*. Cambridge.

Schimmelfennig, Frank (2005a): *The EU: Promoting Liberal-Democracy through Membership Conditionality*. In: Trine Flockhart (ed.): *Socializing Democratic Norms: The Role of International Organizations for the Construction of Europe*. Basingstoke, 106-126.

Schimmelfennig, Frank (2005b): *Strategic Calculation and International Socialization: Membership Incentives, Party Constellations, and Sustained Compliance in Central and Eastern Europe*. In: International Organization, 59(4), 827-860.

Schimmelfennig, Frank (2007): *European Regional Organizations, Political Conditionality, and Democratic Transformation in Eastern Europe*. In: East European Politics and Societies, 21(1), 126-141.

Schimmelfennig, Frank (2008): *EU political accession conditionality after the 2004 enlargement: consistency and effectiveness*. In: Journal of European Public Policy, 15(6), 918-937.

Schimmelfennig, Frank (2009): *Europeanization beyond Europe*. In: Living Reviews in European Governance, 4(3), 17 December 2009.
http://europeangovernance.livingreviews.org/Articles/lreg-2009-3
(accessed on 27 August 2010).

Schimmelfennig, Frank / Engert, Stefan / Knobel, Heiko (2003): *Costs, Commitment, and Compliance. The Impact of EU Democratic Conditionality on Latvia, Slovakia, and Turkey*. In: Journal of Common Market Studies 41(3), 495-518.

Schimmelfennig, Frank / Engert, Stefan / Knobel, Heiko (2006): *International Socialization in Europe: European Organizations, Political Conditionality and Democratic Change*. Basingstoke.

Schimmelfennig, Frank / Scholtz, Hanno (2008): *EU Democracy Promotion in the European Neighbourhood: Political Conditionality, Economic Development and Transnational Exchange*. In: European Union Politics, 9(2), 187-215.

Schimmelfennig, Frank / Sedelmeier, Ulrich (2002): *Theorizing EU enlargement: research focus, hypotheses, and the state of research*. In: Journal of European Public Policy, 9(4), 500-528.

Schimmelfennig, Frank / Sedelmeier, Ulrich (2004): *Governance by conditionality: EU rule transfer to the candidate countries of Central and Eastern Europe*. In: Journal of European Public Policy, 11(4), 661-679.

Schimmelfennig, Frank / Sedelmeier, Ulrich (eds.) (2005a): *The Europeanization of Central and Eastern Europe*. Ithaca, New York.

Schimmelfennig, Frank / Sedelmeier, Ulrich (2005b): *Introduction: Conceptualizing the Europeanization of Central and Eastern Europe*. In: Frank Schimmelfennig / Ulrich Sedelmeier (eds.): *The Europeanization of Central and Eastern Europe*. Ithaca, New York, 1-28.

Schimmelfennig, Frank / Sedelmeier, Ulrich (2005c): *Conclusions: The Impact of the EU on the Accession Countries*. In: Frank Schimmelfennig / Ulrich Sedelmeier, Ulrich (eds.) (2005): *The Europeanization of Central and Eastern Europe*. Ithaca, New York: 210-228.

Schimmelfennig, Frank / Sedelmeier, Ulrich (2005d): *The politics of EU enlargement: Theoretical and comparative perspectives*. In: Frank Schimmelfennig / Ulrich Sedelmeier (eds.): *The Politics of European Union Enlargement: Theoretical Approaches*. London, 3-29.

Schimmelfennig, Frank / Trauner, Florian (eds.) 2009: *Post-accession compliance in the EU's new member states*. In: European Integration online Papers (EIoP), 13(2). http://eiop.or.at/eiop/texte/EIoP_2009_SpecIssue_2.pdf (accessed on 27 August 2010).

Schraeder, Peter (2003): *The State of the Art in International Democracy Promotion: Results of a Joint European–North American Research Network*. In: Democratization, 10(2), 21-44.

Schwellnus, Guido (2005): *The Adoption of Nondiscrimination and Minority Protection Rules in Romania, Hungary and Poland*. In: Frank Schimmelfennig / Ulrich Sedelmeier (eds): *The Europeanization of Central and Eastern Europe*. Ithaca, New York, 51-70.

Sebastian, Sofia (2008): *The Stabilisation and Association Process: are EU inducements failing in the Western Balkans?* FRIDE Working Paper, No. 53, February 2008, Fundación para las Relaciones Internacionales y el Diálogo Exterior (FRIDE), Madrid. http://www.fride.org/publication/356/the-stabilisation-and-association-process-are-eu-inducements-failing-in-the-western-balkans (accessed on 27 August 2010).

Sedelmeier, Ulrich (2006): *Europeanisation in new member and candidate states*. In: Living Reviews in European Governance, 1(3). http://europeangovernance.livingreviews.org/Articles/lreg-2006-3 (accessed on 27 August 2010).

Sjursen, Helene/Smith, Karen (2004*): Justifying EU foreign policy: the logics underpinning EU enlargement*. In: Ben Tonra / Thomas Christiansen (eds.): *Rethinking European Union foreign policy*, Manchester, 126-141

Snow, David / Benford, Robert (1988): *Ideology, Frame Resonance, and Participant Mobilization*. In: International Social Movement Research, 1, 197-217.

Snow, David / Rochford, Burke / Worden, Steven / Benford, Robert (1986): *Frame Alignment Processes, Micromobilization, and Movement Participation*. In: American Sociological Review, 51(4), 464-481.

Subotić, Jelena (2009): *The Paradox of International Justice Compliance*. In: The International Journal of Transitional Justice, 3(3), 362-383.

Trauner, Florian (2009): *From membership conditionality to policy conditionality: EU external governance in South Eastern Europe*. In: Journal of European Public Policy, 16(5), 774-790.

Treib, Oliver / Falkner, Gerda (2008): *Conclusions: The State of EU Social Standards in Central and Eastern European Practice*. In: Gerda Falkner / Oliver Treib / Elisabeth Holzleithner (eds.): *Compliance in the Enlarged European Union: Living Rights or Dead Letters?* Aldershot / Burlington, 157-181.

Tull, Stephen (2003): *The European Union and Croatia: negotiating "Europeanization" amid national, regional and international interests*. In: Paul Kubicek (ed.): *The European Union and Democratization*. London, 132-149.

Tsebelis, George (2002): *Veto players: how political institutions work*. Princeton.

Uzelak, Gordana (1997): *Franjo Tudjman's Nationalist Ideology*. In: East European Quarterly, 31(4), 449-472.

Weber, Katja / Smith, Michael / Baun, Michael (eds.) (2007): *Governing Europe's Neighbourhood: Partners or Periphery?* Manchester.

Wendt, Alexander (1999): *Social Theory of International Politics*. Cambridge.

White, George (2006): *Serbian Mental Space and National Identity*. In: Valeria Heuberger / Elisabeth Vyslonzil (eds.): *Serbia in Europe: Neighbourhood Relations and European Integration*. Vienna / Berlin, 21-40.

Wichmann, Nina (2007): *Democratisation Without Societal Participation? The European Union as an external actor in the democratisation processes of Serbia and Croatia*. Berlin.

Vachudova, Milada (2005): *Europe Undivided: Democracy, Leverage, and Integration After Communism*. Oxford.

Waltz, Kenneth (1959): *Man, the State and War*. New York.

Whitehead, Alfred (1933): *Adventure of ideas*. Cambridge.

Whitehead, Laurence (2004): *Democratization with the benefit of hindsight: The changing international components*. In: Edward Newman / Roland Rich (eds.): *The UN Role in Promoting Democracy: Between Ideals and Reality*. Tokyo / New York, 135-165.

Yilmaz, Hakan (2002): *External-Internal Linkages in Democratization: Developing an Open Model of Democratic Change*. In: Democratization, 9(2), 67-84.

Yin, Robert (2009): *Case study research: design and methods*. Thousand Oaks, California.

Youngs, Richard (2001): *European Union Democracy Promotion Policies: Ten Years On*. In: European Foreign Affairs Review, 6(3), 355-373.

Youngs, Richard (ed.) (2008): *Is the European Union Supporting Democracy in its Neighbourhood?* Fundación para las Relaciones Internacionales y el Diálogo Exterior (FRIDE), September 2008, Madrid.
http://www.fride.org/download/librofride.pdf
(accessed on 26 August 2010).

Youngs, Richard (2009): *Democracy promotion as external governance?* In: Journal of European Public Policy, 16(6), 895-915.

Zakošek, Nenad (2007): *The Heavy Burden of History: Political Uses of the Past in the Yugoslav Successor States.* In: Politička misao, XLIV(5), 29-43.

Zakošek, Nenad (2008): *Democratization, State-building and War: The Cases of Serbia and Croatia.* In: Democratization, 15(3), 588-610.

Žanić, Ivo (2005): The Symbolic Identity of Croatia in the Triangle *Crossroads Bulwark Bridge*. In: Pål Kolstø (ed.): *Myths and Boundaries in South-Eastern Europe*, London, 35-76.

Žanić, Ivo (2007): *Flag on the mountain: a political anthropology of the war in Croatia and Bosnia-Herzegovina 1990 – 1995.* London.

Zürn, Michael / Checkel, Jeffrey (2005): *Getting Socialized to Build Bridges: Constructivism and Rationalism, Europe and the Nation-State.* In: International Organization, 59(4), 1045-1079.

7.2 Documents

7.2.1 European Union documents

Commission (1997): *Agenda 2000: For a stronger and wider European Union.* Document drawn up on the basis of COM(97) 2000 final, EU Bulletin Supplement 5-1997, 15 July 1997.
http://aei.pitt.edu/3137/01/000033.PDF
(accessed on 27 August 2010).

Commission (2000): *Report from the Commission on the feasibility negotiating a Stabilisation and Association Agreement with the Republic of Croatia.* COM(2000) 311 final, 24 May 2000, Brussels.
http://eur-lex.europa.eu/LexUriServ/LexUriServ.do?uri=COM:2000:0311:FIN:EN:PDF
(accessed on 3 September 2010).

Commission (2003): *Communication from the Commission to the Council and the European Parliament: Wider Europe— Neighbourhood: A New Framework for Relations with our Eastern and Southern Neighbours.* COM(2003) 104 final, 11 March 2003, Brussels.
http://ec.europa.eu/world/enp/pdf/com03_104_en.pdf (accessed on 3 September 2010).

Commission (2004a): *Serbia and Montenegro Stabilisation and Association Report 2004.* Commission Staff Working Paper, SEC(2004) 376, no date given, Brussels.
http://ec.europa.eu/enlargement/archives/pdf/serbia_and_montenegro/cr_s-m_en.pdf
(accessed on 3 September 2010).

Commission (2004b): *Communication from the Commission: Opinion on Croatia's Application for Membership of the European Union*. COM(2004) 257 final, 20 April 2004, Brussels.
http://eur-lex.europa.eu/LexUriServ/LexUriServ.do?uri=COM:2004:0257:FIN:EN:PDF (accessed on 3 September 2010).

Commission (2005a): *Communication from the Commission: 2005 Enlargement Strategy Paper*. COM(2005) 561 final, 9 November 2005, Brussels.
http://eur-lex.europa.eu/LexUriServ/LexUriServ.do?uri=COM:2005:0561:FIN:EN:PDF (accessed on 3 September 2010).

Commission (2005b): *Croatia 2005 Progress Report*. SEC (2005) 1424, 9 November 2005, Brussels.
http://ec.europa.eu/enlargement/archives/pdf/key_documents/2005/package/sec_1424_final_progress_report_hr_en.pdf
(accessed on 3 September 2010).

Commission (2006): *Communication by the European Commission to the European Parliament and the Council: Enlargement Strategy and Main Challenges 2006 – 2007 Including annexed special report on the EU's capacity to integrate new members*. COM(2006) 649 final, 8 November 2006, Brussels.
http://ec.europa.eu/enlargement/pdf/key_documents/2006/Nov/com_649_strategy_paper_en.pdf
(accessed on 3 September 2010).

Commission (2007a): *Croatia 2007 Progress Report accompanying the Communication from the Commission to the European Parliament and the Council: Enlargement Strategy and Main Challenges 2007-2008*. Commission Staff Working Document, SEC(2007) 1431, 6 November 2007, Brussels.
http://ec.europa.eu/enlargement/pdf/key_documents/2007/nov/croatia_progress_reports_en.pdf
(accessed on 3 September 2010).

Commission (2007b): *Serbia 2007 Progress Report accompanying the Communication from the Commission to the European Parliament and the Council: Enlargement Strategy and Main Challenges 2007-2008*. Commission Staff Working Document, SEC(2007) 1435, 6 November 2007, Brussels.
http://ec.europa.eu/enlargement/pdf/key_documents/2007/nov/serbia_progress_reports_en.pdf
(accessed on 3 September 2010).

Commission (2008): *Croatia Progress Report 2008: accompanying the Communication from the Commission to the European Parliament and the Council: Enlargement Strategy and Main Challenges 2008-2009*. Commission Staff Working Document, SEC(2008) 2694, 5 November 2008, Brussels.
http://ec.europa.eu/enlargement/pdf/press_corner/keydocuments/reports_nov_2008/croatia_progress_report_en.pdf
(accessed on 3 September 2010).

Commission (2009a): *Croatia Progress Report 2009: accompanying the Communication from the Commission to the European Parliament and the Council: Enlargement Strategy*

and Main Challenges 2009-2010. Commission Staff Working Document, COM(2009) 13333, 14 October 2009, Brussels.
http://ec.europa.eu/enlargement/pdf/key_documents/2009/hr_rapport_2009_en.pdf (accessed on 3 September 2010).

Commission (2009b): *Croatia Progress Report 2009: accompanying the Communication from the Commission to the European Parliament and the Council: Enlargement Strategy and Main Challenges 2009-2010*. Commission Staff Working Document, COM(2009) 533, 14 October 2009, Brussels.
http://ec.europa.eu/enlargement/pdf/key_documents/2009/hr_rapport_2009_en.pdf (accessed on 4 September 2010).

Council of the European Union (2000): *Council Regulation (EC) No. 2666/2000 of 5 December 2000 on assistance for Albania, Bosnia and Herzegovina, Croatia, the Federal Republic of Yugoslavia and the Former Yugoslav Republic of Macedonia, repealing Regulation (EC) No 1628/96 and amending Regulations (EEC) No 3906/89 and (EEC) No 1360/90 and Decisions 97/256/EC and 1999/311/EC*. OJ L 306/1, 7 December 2000, Brussels.
http://eur-lex.europa.eu/LexUriServ/LexUriServ.do?uri=OJ:L:2000:306:0001:0006:EN:PDF (accessed on 27 August 2010).

Council of the European Union (2003): *General Affairs and External Relations: 2518th Council meeting: External relations*. 10369/03 (Presse 166), 16 June 2003, Luxembourg.
http://www.consilium.europa.eu/ueDocs/cms_Data/docs/pressdata/en/gena/76201.pdf (accessed on 27 August 2010).

Council of the European Union (2005): *Council Conclusions of 16 March 2005*. Press Release No. 6969/05 (Presse 44), 16 March 2005, Brussels.
http://ec.europa.eu/external_relations/gac/date/2005/03_160305_ga.pdf (accessed on 3 September 2010).

Council of the European Union (2006a): *Press Release: 2712th Council Meeting General Affairs and External Relations External Relations*. Press Release No. 6344/06 (Presse 46), 27 February 2006, Brussels.
http://www.consilium.europa.eu/uedocs/cms_data/docs/pressdata/en/gena/88541.pdf (accessed on 27 August 2010).

Council of the European Union (2006b): *Council Regulation (EC) No. 1085/2006 of 17 July 2006 establishing an Instrument for Pre-Accession Assistance (IPA)*. OJ L 210, 31 July 2006.
http://eur-lex.europa.eu/LexUriServ/LexUriServ.do?uri=CELEX:32006R1085:EN:NOT (accessed on 27 August 2010).

Council of the European Union (2008): *Press Release: 2678th Council Meeting General Affairs and External Relations General Affairs: Luxembourg, 3 October 2005*. 12514/1/05 REV 1 (en, nl, da, fi) (Presse 241), 3 October 2005, Luxemburg.
http://www.consilium.europa.eu/uedocs/cms_Data/docs/pressdata/en/gena/86442.pdf (accessed on 3 September 2010).

European Council (1993): *European Council in Copenhagen 21-22 June 1993: Conclusions of the Presidency*. OJ SN 180/93 REV 1, 21-22 June 1993, Copenhagen.

http://www.consilium.europa.eu/ueDocs/cms_Data/docs/pressData/en/ec/72921.pdf (accessed on 27 August 2010).

European Council (1996): *Council Conclusions and Declaration on Former Yugoslavia*, adopted by the Council on 26 February 1996, Bulletin EU 1/2-1996, point 1.4.108, 26 February 1996.
http://europa.eu/archives/bulletin/en/9601/p104108.htm
(accessed on 4 September 2010).

European Council (1997): *Council conclusions on the principle of conditionality governing the development of the European Union's relations with certain countries of south-east Europe*. Bulletin EU 4-1997, point 2.2.1 Annex I, 29 April 1997, Brussels.
http://europa.eu/archives/bulletin/en/9704/p202001.htm#anch0514
(accessed on 27 August 2010).

European Council (1999): *Common Position of 17 May 1999 adopted by the Council on the basis of Article 15 of the Treaty on European Union, concerning a Stability Pact for South-Eastern Europe*. 1999/345/CFSP), OJ 1999 L 133/1, 17 May 1999, Brussels.
http://eur-lex.europa.eu/LexUriServ/LexUriServ.do?uri=OJ:L:1999:133:0001:0002:EN:PDF
(accessed on 27 August 2010).

European Council (2000): *Presidency Conclusions Santa Maria da Feira European Council 19 and 20 June 2000*. Bulletin EU 6-2000, points I.2-I.58, 19-20 June 2000, Santa Maria da Feira.
http://europa.eu/archives/bulletin/en/200006/i1001.htm#anch0002
(accessed on 27 August 2010).

European Council (2003): *Presidency Conclusions of the Thessaloniki European Council 19 and 20 June 2003*. Bulletin EU 06-2003, points I.2-I.56, 19-20 June 1999, Thessaloniki.
http://europa.eu/archives/bulletin/en/200306/i1001.htm#anch0002
(accessed on 27 August 2010).

European Council (2004a): *Presidency Conclusions: Brussels European Council 17 and 18 June 2004*. Bulletin EU 6-2004, points I.2-I.29, 17 and 18 June 2004, Brussels.
http://europa.eu/archives/bulletin/en/200406/i1001.htm#anch0002
(accessed on 27 August 2010).

European Council (2004b): *Presidency Conclusions: Brussels European Council 17 and 18 December 2004*. Bulletin EU 12-2004, points I.2-I.25, 17 and 18 July 2004, Brussels.
http://europa.eu/archives/bulletin/en/200412/i1001.htm
(accessed on 4 September 2010).

European Council (2004c): *Presidency Conclusions of the Brussels European Council 16 and 17 December 2004*. Bulletin EU 12-2004, points I.2-I.25, December 2004, Brussels.
http://europa.eu/archives/bulletin/en/200412/i1001.htm#anch0002
(accessed on 4 September 2010).

7.2.2 Documents of the United Nations (UN)

UNDP (2006): *Transitional Justice: Assessment Survey of Conditions in the Former-Yugoslavia*. United Nations Development Programme (UNDP), June 2006, Belgrade. http://www.undp.org/cpr/documents/jssr/trans_justice/UNDP_2006_Balkans_Transitional_Justice_Assessment.pdf (accessed on 3 September 2010).

UNSC (1996): *Letter dated 16 September 1996 from the President of the International Tribunal for the Prosecution of Persons Responsible for Serious Violations of International Humanitarian Law Committed in the Territory of the Former Yugoslavia since 1991 addressed to the President of the Security Council*. United Nations Security Council (UNSC), S/1996/763, 17 September 1996, New York. http://seagrass.goatchurch.org.uk/~undemocracy/cgi-bin/web2/trunk.py/S-1996-763.pdf (accessed on 3 September 2010).

UNSC (1999): *Letter dated 2 November 1999 from the President of the International Tribunal for the Prosecution of Persons Responsible for Serious Violations of International Humanitarian Law Committed in the Territory of the Former Yugoslavia since 1991 addressed to the President of the Security Council*. United Nations Security Council (UNSC), S/1999/1117, 2 November 1999, New York. http://daccess-ddsny. un.org/doc/UNDOC/GEN/N99/326/18/PDF/N9932618.pdf?OpenElement (accessed on 3 September 2010).

UNSC (2001): *Eighth annual report of the International Tribunal for the Prosecution of Persons Responsible for Serious Violations of International Humanitarian Law Committed in the Territory of the Former Yugoslavia since 1991*. A/56/352–S/2001/865, United Nations Security Council (UNSC), 17 September 2001, New York. http://www.icty.org/x/file/About/Reports%20and%20Publications/AnnualReports/annual_report_2001_en.pdf (accessed on 3 September 2010).

UNSC (2002): *Ninth annual report of the International Tribunal for the Prosecution of Persons Responsible for Serious Violations of International Humanitarian Law Committed in the Territory of the Former Yugoslavia since 1991*. A/57/379–S/2002/985, United Nations Security Council (UNSC), 4 September 2002, Ney York. http://www.icty.org/x/file/About/Reports%20and%20Publications/AnnualReports/annual_report_2002_en.pdf (accessed on 3 September 2010).

UNSC (2003): *Tenth annual report of the International Tribunal for the Prosecution of Persons Responsible for Serious Violations of International Humanitarian Law Committed in the Territory of the Former Yugoslavia since 1991*. A/58/297–S/2003/829, United Nations Security Council (UNSC), 20 August 2003, New York. http://www.icty.org/x/file/About/Reports%20and%20Publications/AnnualReports/annual_report_2003_en.pdf (accessed on 3 September 2010).

UNSC (2004): *Eleventh annual report of the International Tribunal for the Prosecution of Persons Responsible for Serious Violations of International Humanitarian Law Committed*

in the Territory of the Former Yugoslavia since 1991. A/59/215.S/2004/627, United Nations Security Council (UNSC), 16 August 2004, New York.
http://www.icty.org/x/file/About/Reports%20and%20Publications/AnnualReports/annual_report_2004_en.pdf
(accessed on 3 September 2010).

UNSC (2005): *Twelfth annual report of the International Tribunal for the Prosecution of Persons Responsible for Serious Violations of International Humanitarian Law Committed in the Territory of the Former Yugoslavia since 1991.* A/60/267–S/2005/532, United Nations Security Council (UNSC), 17 August 2005, New York.
http://www.icty.org/x/file/About/Reports%20and%20Publications/AnnualReports/annual_report_2005_en.pdf
(accessed on 3 September 2010).

UNSC (2006): *Thirteenth annual report of the International Tribunal for the Prosecution of Persons Responsible for Serious Violations of International Humanitarian Law Committed in the Territory of the Former Yugoslavia since 1991.* A/61/271–S/2006/666, United Nations Security Council (UNSC), 21 August 2006, New York.
http://www.icty.org/x/file/About/Reports%20and%20Publications/AnnualReports/annual_report_2006_en.pdf
(accessed on 3 September 2010).

UNSC (2007): *Fourteenth annual report of the International Tribunal for the Prosecution of Persons Responsible for Serious Violations of International Humanitarian Law Committed in the Territory of the Former Yugoslavia since 1991.* A/62/172–S/2007/469, United Nations Security Council, 1 August 2007, New York.
http://www.icty.org/x/file/About/Reports%20and%20Publications/AnnualReports/annual_report_2007_en.pdf
(accessed on 4 September 2010).

UNSC (2008): *Fifteenth annual report of the International Tribunal for the Prosecution of Persons Responsible for Serious Violations of International Humanitarian Law Committed in the Territory of the Former Yugoslavia since 1991.* A/63/210–S/2008/515, United Nations Security Council, 4 August 2008, New York.
http://www.icty.org/x/file/About/Reports%20and%20Publications/AnnualReports/annual_report_2008_en.pdf
(accessed on 4 September 2010).

UNSC (2009): Sixteenth annual report of the International Tribunal for the Prosecution of Persons Responsible for Serious Violations of International Humanitarian Law Committed in the Territory of the Former Yugoslavia since 1991. A/64/205–S/2009/394, United Nations Security Council, 31 July 2009, New York.
http://www.icty.org/x/file/About/Reports%20and%20Publications/AnnualReports/annual_report_2009_en.pdf
(accessed on 4 September 2010).

7.3 Media reports

AFP (2001): *Croatia's Cooperation With the UN War Crimes Tribunal: A Timeline of Developments*. Agence France-Presse (AFP), 16 July 2001.
http://www.globalpolicy.org/component/content/article/163/28769.html
(accessed on 1 September 2010).

BBC (1999): *No extradition for Croatian generals*. British Broadcasting Corporation (BBC), BBC News, written by Gabriel Partos, 18 October 1999.
http://news.bbc.co.uk/2/hi/europe/478647.stm
(accessed on 1 September 2010).

BBC (2000): *Croatia votes for war crimes trials*. British Broadcasting Corporation (BBC), BBC News, 15 April 2000.
http://news.bbc.co.uk/2/hi/europe/714068.stm
(accessed on 1 September 2010).

BBC (2001a): *Croatians rally to war crimes suspect*. British Broadcasting Corporation (BBC), BBC News, 11 February 2001.
http://news.bbc.co.uk/2/hi/world/monitoring/media_reports/1164457.stm
(accessed on 1 September 2010).

BBC (2001b): *Croatian Protesters Lift Blockade*. British Broadcasting Corporation (BBC), BBC News, 12 February 2001.
http://news.bbc.co.uk/2/hi/europe/1166864.stm
(accessed on 1 September 2010).

BBC (2001c): *Croatia awaits protests*. British Broadcasting Corporation (BBC), BBC World News, 9 July 2001.
http://news.bbc.co.uk/2/hi/europe/1429912.stm
(accessed on 1 September 2010).

BBC (2003a): *US Reward for Croatian Fugitive*. British Broadcasting Corporation (BBC), BBC News, 8 October 2003.
http://news.bbc.co.uk/2/hi/europe/3178836.stm
(accessed on 1 September 2010).

BBC (2003b): *Germany backs Croatia's EU bid*. British Broadcasting Corporation (BBC), BBC News, 30 October 2003.
http://news.bbc.co.uk/2/hi/europe/3228405.stm
(accessed on 1 September 2010).

BBC (2003c): *New Croatian cabinet is approved*. British Broadcasting Corporation (BBC), BBC News, 23 December 2003.
http://news.bbc.co.uk/2/hi/europe/3339851.stm
(accessed on 1 September 2010).

BBC (2004a): *Croatia's EU future*. British Broadcasting Corporation (BBC), BBC News, HARDtalk interview with Miomir Žužul, 13 February 2004.
http://news.bbc.co.uk/go/pr/fr/-/2/hi/programmes/hardtalk/3486367.stm
(accessed on 1 September 2010).

BBC (2004b): *Croatian generals to surrender*. British Broadcasting Corporation (BBC), BBC News, 8 March 2004.
http://news.bbc.co.uk/2/hi/europe/3542757.stm
(accessed on 1 September 2010).

BBC (2005a): *Del Ponte takes swipe at Croatia*. British Broadcasting Corporation (BBC), BBC News, 17 February 2005.
http://news.bbc.co.uk/2/hi/europe/4274269.stm
(accessed on 1 September 2010).

BBC (2005b): *MI6 and the Croatian general*. British Broadcasting Corporation (BBC), BBC News, written by Nick Thorpe, 30 April 2005.
http://news.bbc.co.uk/2/hi/programmes/from_our_own_correspondent/4497385.stm
(accessed on 1 September 2010).

BBC (2005c): *Croatia's spybusters uncovered*. British Broadcasting Corporation (BBC), BBC News, written by Tim Whewell, 2 June 2005.
http://news.bbc.co.uk/2/hi/programmes/newsnight/4603991.stm
(accessed on 1 September 2010).

BBC (2005d): *Hungary backs Croatia in EU spat*. British Broadcasting Corporation (BBC), BBC News, written by Nick Thorpe, 14 April 2005.
http://news.bbc.co.uk/2/hi/europe/4444885.stm
(accessed on 1 September 2010).

BBC (2005e): *EU opens Turkey membership talks*. British Broadcasting Corporation (BBC), BBC News, 4 October 2005.
http://news.bbc.co.uk/2/hi/europe/4305500.stm
(accessed on 1 September 2010).

BBC (2005f): *Shock, awe and exhaustion*. British Broadcasting Corporation (BBC), BBC News, 4 October 2005, written by Jonny Dymond, 4 October 2005.
http://news.bbc.co.uk/2/hi/europe/4309762.stm
(accessed on 1 September 2010).

BBC (2008a): *Why Bosnia's most wanted run free*. British Broadcasting Corporation (BBC), BBC News, 28 June 2008.
http://news.bbc.co.uk/2/hi/programmes/from_our_own_correspondent/7477912.stm
(accessed on 1 September 2010).

BBC (2008b): *The hunt for Karadzic and Mladic*. British Broadcasting Corporation (BBC), BBC News, 23 July 2008.
http://news.bbc.co.uk/2/hi/europe/4079642.stm
(accessed on 1 September 2010).

Central Europe Review (2000a): *News from Croatia: All the important news since 8 April 2000*. Written by Saša Cvijetić, 2(15), 17 April 2000.
http://www.ce-review.org/00/15/croatianews15.html
(accessed on 1 September 2010).

Central Europe Review (2000b): *News from Croatia: All the important news since 2 October 2000: Letter sparks coup rumours*. Written by Pat FitzPatrick, 2(34), 9 October 2000. http://www.ce-review.org/00/34/croatianews34.html (accessed on 1 September 2010).

Central Europe Review (2001): *News from Croatia: All the important news since 19 February 2001*. Written by Dan Damon, 3(8), 26 February 2001. http://www.ce-review.org/01/8/croatianews8.html (accessed on 1 September 2010).

CNN (2001a): *Croatia in war crimes crisis*. Cable News Network (CNN), 9 July 2001. http://archives.cnn.com/2001/WORLD/europe/07/08/croatia.crisis (accessed on 1 September 2010).

CNN (2001b): *Croat general to surrender*. Cable News Network (CNN), 13 July 2001. http://archives.cnn.com/2001/WORLD/europe/07/13/croat.warcrim/index.html (accessed on 1 September 2010).

CNN (2005): *Croatian war suspect flown to Hague*. Cable News Network (CNN), 12 December 2005. http://www.cnn.com/2005/WORLD/europe/12/10/croatia.suspect/index.html?iref=allsearch (accessed on 1 September 2010).

Financial Times (2005a): *President wins second term in Croatia by big margin*. Written by Eric Jansson, 17 January 2005. http://www.ft.com/cms/s/0/df443ed2-682d-11d9-a11e-00000e2511c8.html (accessed on 1 September 2010).

Financial Times (2005b): *Croatia tries to allay EU concern over war suspect*. Written by Daniel Dombey, 2 March 2005. http://www.ft.com/cms/s/0/3858183c-8b41-11d9-ae03-00000e2511c8.html (accessed on 1 September 2010).

Financial Times (2005c): *Austria claims 'double standards' on Turkish talks*. Written by Haig Simonian, Daniel Dombey, Raphael Minder, 29 September 2005. http://www.ft.com/cms/s/0/23b0c7fe-3086-11da-ba9f-00000e2511c8.html (accessed on 1 September 2010).

Financial Times (2005d): *European Union must square up to Croatia on charges against Gotovina*. In: Financial Times, 30 September 2005. http://www.ft.com/cms/s/0/7e125398-314e-11da-ac1b-00000e2511c8.html (accessed on 3 September 2010).

NYT (1999): *Snubbed by the West, Tudjman Receives a Posthumous Rebuke*. The New York Times (NYT), written by Steven Erlanger, 14 December 1999. http://www.nytimes.com/1999/12/14/world/snubbed-by-the-west-tudjman-receives-a-posthumous-rebuke.html?scp=9&sq=erlanger&st=nyt&pagewanted=print (accessed on 1 September 2010).

NYT (2000a): *Opposition Ex-Communist favored in Croatia Vote*. The New York Times (NYT), written by Steven Erlanger, 1 January 2000.

http://www.nytimes.com/2000/01/01/world/opposition-ex-communist-favored-in-croatia-vote.html?scp=10&sq=erlanger&st=nyt
(accessed on 1 September 2010).

NYT (2000b): *Pro-Western Opposition Defeats Croatia's Ruling Nationalists*. The New York Times (NYT), written by Steven Erlanger, 5 January 2000.
http://www.nytimes.com/2000/01/05/world/pro-western-opposition-defeats-croatia-s-ruling-nationalists.html?scp=11&sq=erlanger&st=nyt&pagewanted=print
(accessed on 1 September 2010).

NYT (2000c): *Croatian Victors Fret About What Awaits Them*. The New York Times (NYT), written by Steven Erlanger, 6 January 2000.
http://www.nytimes.com/2000/01/06/world/croatian-victors-fret-about-what-awaits-them.html?scp=6&sq=erlanger&st=nyt
(accessed on 1 September 2010).

NYT (2000d): *Albright Visits Post-Tudjman Croatia and Hails the New Leadership*. The New York Times (NYT), written by Steven Erlanger, 3 February 2000.
http://www.nytimes.com/2000/02/03/world/albright-visits-post-tudjman-croatia-and-hails-the-new-leadership.html?scp=1&sq=steven+erlanger+albright&st=nyt
(accessed on 1 September 2010).

NYT (2000e): *Croatia Elects a Moderate to Follow the Tudjman Era*. The New York Times (NYT), written by Steven Erlanger, 8 February 2000.
http://www.nytimes.com/2000/02/08/world/croatia-elects-a-moderate-to-follow-the-tudjman-era.html
(accessed on 1 September 2010).

NYT (2001a): *Croatian Rally Protests U.N. And Demands Early Elections*. The New York Times (NYT), 12 February 2001.
http://www.nytimes.com/2001/02/12/world/croatian-rally-protests-un-and-demands-early-elections.html?scp=1&sq=croatian%20rally%20protests%2012%20february%202001&st=cse (accessed on 1 September 2010).

NYT (2001b): *Croatia in Turmoil After Agreeing to Send 2 to Tribunal*. The New York Times (NYT), written by Carlotta Gall and Marlise Simons, 8 July 2001.
http://www.nytimes.com/2001/07/09/world/croatia-in-turmoil-after-agreeing-to-send-2-to-tribunal.html?scp=1&sq=del+ponte+croatia&st=nyt
(accessed on 1 September 2010).

NYT (2002a): *Croatia: Tribunal Indicts Ex-General*. The New York Times (NYT), World Briefing / Europe, written by Daniel Simpson, 22 September 2002.
http://www.nytimes.com/2002/09/20/world/world-briefing-europe-croatia-tribunal-indicts-ex-general.html?scp=18&sq=Croatia&st=nyt
(accessed on 1 September 2010).

NYT (2002b): *The Hague: Tribunal Demands Croatian General*. The New York Times (NYT), World Briefing / Europe, written by Marlise Simons, 30 November 2002.
http://www.nytimes.com/2002/11/30/world/world-briefing-europe-the-hague-tribunal-demands-croatian-general.html?scp=2&sq=croatia&st=nyt
(accessed on 1 September 2010).

NYT (2002c): *Croatia Protects a General Charged With War Crimes.* The New York Times (NYT), written by Daniel Simpson, 3 December 2002.
http://www.nytimes.com/2002/12/03/world/croatia-protects-a-general-charged-with-war-crimes.html?scp=10&sq=Croatia&st=nyt
(accessed on 1 September 2010).

NYT (2003a): *Croatia: General Too Sick For Trial.* The New York Times (NYT), World Briefing / Europe, written by Daniel Simpson, 6 February 2003.
http://www.nytimes.com/2003/02/06/world/world-briefing-europe-croatia-general-too-sick-for-trial.html?scp=19&sq=Croatia&st=nyt
(accessed on 1 September 2010).

NYT (2003b): *Croatia Waiting for a European Balkans Plan.* The New York Times (NYT), written by Daniel Simpson, 23 February 2003.
http://www.nytimes.com/2003/02/23/world/croatia-waiting-for-a-european-balkans-plan.html?scp=6&sq=Croatia&st=nyt
(accessed on 1 September 2010).

NYT (2003c): *A Fugitive Croatia General Is a Hometown Favorite.* The New York Times (NYT), written by Peter Green, 5 June 2003.
http://www.nytimes.com/2003/06/05/world/a-fugitive-croatia-general-is-a-hometown-favorite.html?scp=5&sq=Croatia&st=nyt
(accessed on 1 September 2010).

NYT (2008): *War Crimes Trial Begins for Croatian General Who Worked With Americans.* The New York Times (NYT), written by Marlise Simons, 12 March 2008.
http://www.nytimes.com/2008/03/12/world/europe/12hague.html?scp=4&sq=croatia_markac&st=cse
(accessed on 1 September 2010).

RFE/RL (2001a): *Croatia: Political Crisis Over Arrest of War Crimes Suspects.* Radio Free Europe / Radio Liberty (RFE/RL), written by Breffini O'Rourke, 9 July 2001.
http://www.rferl.org/content/article/1096880.html
(accessed on 1 September 2010).

RFE/RL (2001b): *Croatia: Government Survives Confidence Vote in Parliament.* Radio Free Europe / Radio Liberty (RFE/RL), written by Jolyon Naegele, 16 July 2001.
http://www.rferl.org/content/article/1096935.html
(accessed on 1 September 2010).

Southeast European Times (2002): *EU Mission Monitor's Croatia's Progress.* 22 October 2002.
http://www.setimes.com/cocoon/setimes/xhtml/en_GB/features/setimes/newsbriefs/2002/10/021022-GEORGI-009
(accessed on 3 September 2010).

The Guardian (2002): *Croatia refuses to hand over general accused of war crimes: Showdown with UN looms after indictment for massacre of Serbs in 1993 is defied.* Written by Ian Traynor, 26 September 2002.
http://www.guardian.co.uk/world/2002/sep/26/warcrimes.unitednations
(accessed on 1 September 2010).

The Guardian (2004a): *MI6 involved in Balkan spy plot, says Croatian paper*. Written by Ian Traynor, 27 August 2004.
http://www.guardian.co.uk/world/2004/aug/27/balkans.warcrimes
(accessed on 1 September 2010).

The Guardian (2004b): *War crimes cause EU rift over Croatia*. Written by Ian Traynor. 9 December 2004.
http://www.guardian.co.uk/world/2004/dec/09/eu.warcrimes
(accessed on 1 September 2010).

The Guardian (2005a): *Find fugitive general within 10 days or forget your EU ambitions, Croatia told*. Written by Ian Traynor, 7 March 2005.
http://www.guardian.co.uk/world/2005/mar/07/eu.warcrimes
(accessed on 1 September 2010).

The Guardian (2005b): *EU delays Croatia entry talks over missing general*. 16 March 2005.
http://www.guardian.co.uk/world/2005/mar/16/warcrimes.eu
(accessed on 1 September 2010).

The Guardian (2005c): *The fugitive who stands in the way of Croatia's EU entry*. Written by Ian Traynor, 18 March 2005.
http://www.guardian.co.uk/world/2005/mar/18/eu.warcrimes
(accessed on 1 September 2010).

The Guardian (2005d): *EU warns Austria on Turks*. Written by Nicholas Watt, 1 October 2005.
http://www.guardian.co.uk/world/2005/oct/01/turkey.eu
(accessed on 1 September 2010).

The Guardian (2005e): *Capture of war crimes suspect paves Croatia's way to EU entry*. Written by Ian Traynor and Giles Tremlett, 9 December 2005.
http://www.guardian.co.uk/world/2005/dec/09/warcrimes.eu
(accessed on 1 September 2010).

The Guardian (2005f): *War crimes suspect was using a false passport*. 10 December 2005.
http://www.guardian.co.uk/world/2005/dec/10/warcrimes
(accessed on 1 September 2010).

UN Wire (2001): *Cabinet Approves Cooperation With UN Tribunal*. 9 July 2001.
http://www.unwire.org/unwire/20010709/15883_story.asp
(accessed on 27 July 2010).